STO

5.24.79

Acquisition of the Consumer Role by Adolescents

George P. Moschis

Department of Marketing
College of Business Administration
Georgia State University

1978

Research Monograph No. 82

Publishing Services Division
College of Business Administration/Georgia State University
Atlanta, Georgia

Library of Congress Cataloging in Publication Data

Moschis, George P   1944-
    Acquisition of the consumer role by adolescents.

    (Research monograph - College of Business Administration,
Georgia State University ; no. 82)
    Bibliography: p.
    1. Youth as consumers—Wisconsin. 2. Consumer education—
United States. 3. Socialization. I. Title. II. Series: Georgia
State University. College of Business Administration. Research
monograph - College of Business Administration, Georgia
State University ; no. 82.
HC107.W63C615   381'.3   78-10344
ISBN 0-88406-124-8

Published by:
Publishing Services Division
College of Business Administration
Georgia State University
University Plaza
Atlanta, GA 30303

Georgia State University is an equal educational opportunity
institution and an equal opportunity/affirmative action employer.

Cover photograph and design by Richard Shannon

To Nancy

CRITICS

Table of Contents

Acknowledgements

This research was conducted in partial fulfillment of the requirements for the Ph.D. degree in Business at the University of Wisconsin. As a result, there are a number of individuals who made this study possible and whose assistance I would like to recognize.

I am indebted to Gil Churchill for providing guidance and constructive criticism throughout the study. He contributed a great deal to this study and made this research effort a very exciting and satisfying learning experience. My sincere gratitude is also extended to Jack McLeod and Ivan Preston, Professors of Journalism and Mass Communication, and to Michael Rothschild and Ron Stampfl, Professors of Business, all of the University of Wisconsin.

My special thanks to Roy Moore, Professor of Journalism at Georgia State, and Steve Chaffee, Professor of Journalism and Mass Communication at the University of Wisconsin. The interactions I had with them during my graduate studies at Wisconsin guided my initial thoughts on this project and made it a better study.

I also thank the American Marketing Association for awarding me a doctoral research grant that encouraged me to develop my initial thoughts into a larger scale project. Bruce Le Grande, Director of the Northern Wisconsin Development Center, also provided financial support for several years. I

x

thank him for letting me work with him and his staff and acquire invaluable experience, which helped me carry out this project.

I thank the many school officials, teachers, and students whose cooperation and participation made this project possible.

Mrs. Beverly Scrag helped me with this project from the beginning. She gave me helpful suggestions and helped me with editing and typing. I thank her for her excellent work, promptness, and patience. Also, I want to thank Ms. Harriett Jones for her invaluable assistance in preparing this monograph.

Finally, to my wife, Nancy, this work is dedicated as a small token of my appreciation for her "suffering" during my graduate studies at Wisconsin, her continuous encouragement, understanding, and support.

—George P. Moschis

Chapter 1

Introduction

Consumer learning among young people is of increasing interest to marketing practitioners, public policy makers, consumer educators, and students of consumer behavior. This area is important from the marketer's point of view for several reasons. Some of the main reasons are that young people make up a large specialized segment of the market for many goods and they influence family and peer spending patterns. One recent tally, for example, estimated the annual youth market at $3.5 billion discretionary income, $45 billion spending, and $145 billion influential spending.[1] In addition, experiences of youths that are related to consumption presumably affect their consumption patterns as adults. For instance, individuals are likely to maintain through adulthood brand and product preferences they developed as young people.[2]

Consumer learning by young people also appears to be of interest to public policy makers. Major concerns at the 1971 Federal Trade Commission (FTC) hearings, for example, were the effects of television advertising on consumer learning and, generally, the processes by which young people develop consumption-related attitudes, skills, and behaviors.[3]

Consumer educators also have been interested in understanding the processes by which young people acquire consumption-related skills as a means of preparing young people to evaluate and process marketing information. Evidence of this interest is seen in the growing number of states that have recently included consumer education classes in their curricula.[4]

Finally, research in the development of consumer behavior should be of interest to students of consumer behavior. A belief widely held among behavioral scientists is that childhood and adolescent experiences are of paramount importance in shaping later patterns of adult behavior.[5] As one authority on the topic recently put it:

> At least some patterns of adult consumer behavior are influenced by childhood and adolescent experiences, and the study of these experiences should help us understand not only consumer behavior among young people, but the development of adult patterns of behavior as well.[6]

Statement of the Problem

Although there is a growing interest in the consumer behavior of young people and in the processes by which they acquire consumer-related cognitions and behaviors, little information is available to answer the increasing number of questions related to corporate and public policy formulation in regard to consumer learning.[7] One issue of concern is the effect of marketing practices, particularly television advertising, on young people's development of consumer behavior, values, and attitudes. Also of concern is the effect such marketing practices might have on parent-child relationships. Critics, for example, argue that advertising strongly influences the young and results in undesirable socialization (e.g., materialistic values and the need to consume, nonrational impulse-oriented choices) and intrafamily conflict (e.g., pressure on the child to request his parents to buy the advertised products). On the other hand, defenders of these practices argue that parents modify the impact of advertising and are the main source of influence on the child's consumer-learning process. They state that advertising simply sets up the agenda for positive parent-child interaction and provides a consumption-learning experience for the child.[8]

Another issue concerns the processes by which young people develop their ability to evaluate environmental (mainly commercial) stimuli. For example, some individuals argue that a young person's ability to evaluate marketing stimuli is mainly a matter of cognitive development; others contend that responses to such stimuli, and consumer behavior in general, are second-order consequences of more fundamental aspects of social learning acquired through modeling processes.[9]

Questions also have been raised about the validity of some consumer education materials and practices. For example, some researchers have questioned the content of consumer education materials and argue that consumer education efforts are based on false notions and that children learn very little at school about positive consumer practices.[10] Other researchers argue that for several decades educational materials and programs have emphasized the development of economic competence and that the school has always been the main source of young people's positive consumer behaviors.[11]

Unfortunately, previous research in the area of consumer learning does not provide information significant to understanding consumer socialization, i.e., the development of thinking and behaving patterns that make up consumer behavior. Some sociologists have discussed consumer socialization, but only in the context of general essays and not as theoretical propositions that would stimulate programmatic research.[12] On the other hand, socialization and child-development researchers have ignored consumer learning and behavior among young people; instead they have focused on more fundamental social orientations, such as the sex role and moral development of the young person.[13]

Typical research in consumer learning is of two types: research that examines consumer-related communication processes and research that examines consumption-related variables. Research examining communication processes, in turn, concentrates on two kinds of communication processes: family consumer processes and media use. Research examining family consumer processes, however, usually is limited to consideration of husband-wife dyads.[14] Little systematic research exists concerning how the role of parent-child interactions affects consumer-learning processes.[15] Research examining media use has focused almost exclusively on the effects of television programming (e.g., violence) to the virtual exclusion of the effects of television advertising.

Although many studies have been conducted on the effects of advertising, the majority have been concerned with adults rather than with young people.[16] As a result, the effects of advertising on consumer learning are not clear.[17]

Studies focusing on static age groups, on the other hand, have examined a wide variety of variables that are directly related to consumer behavior. Some of these variables are attitudes toward advertising, prices, brands, and saving versus spending.[18] However, the majority of these investigations are rather descriptive and speculative and are not based on sound theoretical grounds.[19] Furthermore, considerably less attention has been devoted to examining variables that are indirectly related to consumer behavior (e.g., motivations for consumption and perceptions of material goods), which can have significant implications for policy and research.[20]

Some recent research examining the developmental patterns of consumer responses to television advertising has concentrated almost exclusively on children[21] but has ignored adolescents, believed to be the most important segment of society for consumer-learning research.[22]

In summary, little systematic research has been developed in the area of consumer socialization. Research is particularly lacking with respect to how consumers learn skills, knowledges, and attitudes. This is information that should be useful to marketing practitioners, public policy makers, consumer educators, and students of consumer behavior. Among such areas of concern are: (1) how specific skills and attitudes that are directly related to consumption (such as the ability to "cognitively filter" puffery in advertising or to evaluate marketing stimuli) are developed; (2) how skills that are indirectly related to consumption (such as motivation for consumption and perceptions of material goods) are developed; (3) what are the processes of learning and what is their relative influence on specific consumption behaviors; and (4) what are the social structural factors that directly affect consumer learning.[23]

Focus of the Study

This research approaches consumer learning from the perspective of the consumer role, that is, the totality of consumer skills, knowledge, and attitudes that contribute to the individual's competence and proficiency as a consumer in the marketplace. It is a large-scale field survey and emphasizes the following:

1. Development of various components or dimensions of the consumer role.

2. Sources of consumer-role acquisition, particularly the influence of parents, mass media, peers, and school.

3. Maturational effects on the acquisition of consumer skills, knowledge, and attitudes. (This research examined maturational effects on consumer-role acquisition in terms of age differences, i.e., younger vs. older adolescents.)

4. Types of skills, knowledge, attitudes, and values learned as a result of different socialization processes.

5. Social structural factors affecting socialization processes and outcomes.

The objectives are to obtain information relevant to contemporary issues, such as the following:

1. What aspects of the consumer role are learned at various ages?

2. How do young people develop consumption-related attitudes, skills, and knowledge?

3. Does the cognitive developmental model of socialization or the social learning model of socialization best explain the development of patterns of thinking and behaving that comprise consumer behavior?

4. What is the relative influence of media, family, peers, and school in the development of specific consumption-related attitudes, skills, knowledge, and motivation?

5. What socialization processes characterize the development of specific consumer skills, such as the ability to cognitively filter puffery in advertising and evaluate marketing stimuli?

6. Do individual differences on social structural variables lead to different socialization processes and, perhaps most important, to different levels of competency on various consumer skills?

This study focuses on adolescence (middle and high school years) because this period is believed to be the most critical period in socialization. Campbell emphasizes the importance of adolescence as a period in socialization by specifying several changes that are likely to occur during the person's life.

For example, he suggests that during this period the individual develops social skills, self-concepts, and conceptions regarding his decisions and their outcomes.[24]

---

1. "Getting Across to the Youth," *Business Week*, October 18, 1969, pp. 89-90.

2. Lester P. Guest, "Brand Loyalty: Twelve Years Later," *Journal of Applied Psychology*, December 1955, pp. 405-408.

3. Action for Children's Television, Testimony before the Federal Trade Commission, November 10, 1971.

4. Paul N. Bloom and Mark J. Silver, "Consumer Education: Marketers Take Heed," *Harvard Business Review*, January-February 1976, pp. 32-42, 149-150; and Scott Ward, "Consumer Socialization," *Journal of Consumer Research*, September 1974, pp. 1-14.

5. Ward, "Consumer Socialization," 1974.

6. Scott Ward, "Consumer Socialization," paper presented to the American Psychological Association Convention, Honolulu, Hawaii, 1972, p. 42.

7. Seymour Banks, Testimony before the Federal Trade Commission, October 28, 1971; Ward, "Consumer Socialization," 1972; and Ward, "Consumer Socialization," 1974.

8. Thomas S. Robertson, "The Impact of Television Advertising on Children," *Wharton Quarterly*, Summer 1972, pp. 38-41.

9. Ward, "Consumer Socialization," 1974.

10. S.L. Diamond, "Consumer Education: Perspectives on the State of the Art," unpublished paper (Cambridge: Harvard University, Graduate School of Business, 1974); Ward, "Consumer Socialization," 1974; and Scott Ward and Daniel B. Wackman, "Effects of Television Advertising on Consumer Socialization," Working Paper (Cambridge, Massachusetts: Marketing Science Institute, 1973).

11. Ruth W. Gavian and Louis C. Nanassy, "Economic Competence as a Goal of Elementary School Education," *Elementary School Journal*, January 1955, pp. 270-273.

12. Ward, "Consumer Socialization," 1974.

13. Ibid.

14. Donald H. Granbois, "The Role of Communication in the Family Decision Making Process," in Stephen A. Greyser, ed., *Toward Scientific Marketing* (Chicago: American Marketing Association, 1964); and Elizabeth H. Wolgast, "Do Husbands or Wives Make the Purchasing Decision?" *Journal of Marketing*, October 1958, pp. 151-158.

15. Roy L. Moore and Lowndes F. Stephens, "Some Communication and Demographic Determinants of Adolescent Consumer Learning," *Journal of Consumer Research*, September 1975, pp. 80-92; and Scott Ward and Daniel B. Wackman, "Family and Media Influences on Adolescent Consumer Learning," *American Behavioral Scientist*, January-February 1971, pp. 415-427.

16. Raymond A. Bauer and Stephen Greyser, *Advertising in America: The Consumer View* (Boston: Harvard Business School, Division of Research, 1968); and Gary A. Steiner, "The People Look at Television," *Journal of Business*, April 1963, pp. 272-304.

17. Moore and Stephens, "Some Communication and Demographic Determinants of Adolescent Consumer Learning"; Ward, "Consumer Socialization," 1974; and Ward and Wackman, "Family and Media Influences on Adolescent Consumer Learning."

18. Philip R. Cateora, *An Analysis of the Teen-age Market* (Austin, Texas: Bureau of Business Research, University of Texas, 1963); Don L. James, *Youth, Media, and Advertising* (Austin, Texas: Bureau of Business Research, University of Texas, 1971); James V. McNeal, *Children as Consumers* (Austin, Texas: Bureau of Business Research, University of Texas, 1965); and Gladys K. Phelan and Jay D. Schvaneveldt, "Spending and Saving Patterns of Adolescent Siblings," *Journal of Home Economics*, February 1969, pp. 104-109.

19. Cateora, *An Analysis of the Teen-age Market*; and McNeal, *Children as Consumers*.

20. Ward, "Consumer Socialization," 1974.

21. Ibid.

22. Earnest Q. Campbell, "Adolescent Socialization," in David A. Goslin, ed., *Handbook of Socialization Theory and Research* (Chicago:

Rand McNally, 1969); and Moore and Stephens, "Some Communication and Demographic Determinants of Adolescent Consumer Learning."

23. Ward, "Consumer Socialization," 1974.

24. Campbell, "Adolescent Socialization," pp. 825-826.

Chapter 2

Background and Hypotheses

Socialization Perspectives

Several approaches can be used to study the socialization of young people to the consumer role.[1] Although no single set of socialization concepts, assumptions, and hypotheses has been agreed upon by all socialization researchers, a rough blueprint does exist outlining what data should be included and what a socialization theory of consumer behavior might look like.

McLeod and O'Keefe maintain that a complete socialization theory must deal with *five* types of variables: (1) *content* or criterion behavior; (2) *agent* or source of the influence; (3) *learning processes* involved in socialization; (4) social structural *constraints* affecting learning; and (5) *age* or life cycle position of the influencee.[2]

Content or Criterion Behavior

Socialization research focuses on the study of the development of learning properties (cognitions and behaviors) necessary for the performance of a given social role. For example, researchers have investigated the socialization of people to social roles such as marital, occupational, and political.[3]

Learning properties can be divided into (1) those properties that help a person function in any given social system and (2) those properties that are related to a person's individual behavior, regardless of the standards set by any larger system.[4] The criteria relevant to the functioning of any given social system are prescribed by that society; they are based on normative theories of human behavior and, in a sense, are efforts on the part of some members of that society to regulate the behavior of other members so that certain "desirable" consequences follow.[5] One general expectation, for example, is that consumers are rational.

Criteria relevant to individual behavior, on the other hand, include cognitions and behaviors that enable the person to enact a given social role, regardless of whether the behaviors are functional or dysfunctional to any larger system. Examples of such consumer learning properties are the various social motivations for consumption, brand and store preferences. Although one cannot entirely ignore gratuitous assumptions about human behavior (e.g., the world would be better off if people conformed to socially prescribed behaviors), it seems particularly useful in socialization research to sort out those behaviors that are defined in terms of their relevance to performing some function for *society* and those cognitions and behaviors defined in terms of their relevance only to the *individual*.[6]

Agent or Source of Influence

Socialization is often viewed as a social process by which norms, attitudes, motivations, and behaviors are transmitted from specific sources, commonly known as "socialization agents," to the learner. "Socialization takes place through interaction of the person and various agents in specific social settings."[7] A socialization agent may be a person or an organization and is directly involved in socialization because of frequency of contact with the individual, primacy over the individual, and control over rewards and punishments given to the individual.[8]

The main implication of including specific influence agents in the socialization model is that the unit of analysis becomes the agent-learner relationship.[9] Tolman classified these agent-to-learner relationships into four categories on the basis of the formality of the type of agent and the role of the learner:

1. Formal organization (agent), role of learner specified. (The best example here is the school.)

2. Formal organization, role of learner not specified (e.g., mass media).

3. Informal organization, role of learner specified (e.g., family).

4. Informal organization, role of learner not specified (e.g., peers).[10]

Learning Processes

The processes by which the learner acquires specific values and behaviors from the socialization agents, while interacting with them, can be divided into three categories: *modeling, reinforcement,* and *social interaction.*

Modeling explanations involve imitation either through a conscious attempt to emulate the socialization agent or because the agent's behavior is the most salient alternative open to the person[11]; for example, a child does the same things his parents do in an effort to be like them. Common operational definitions of modeling processes are correlations between the agent's and child's behavior.[12] This type of learning process has also been referred to as observational and imitation learning.[13]

Reinforcement explanations of learning involve either reward (positive reinforcement) or punishment (negative reinforcement) mechanisms. The person learns to duplicate past behaviors that have been rewarded by the socializing agent and/or to avoid repeating those behaviors for which he has been punished.[14] Among the most common examples of operational definitions of positive and negative reinforcements are parental affection and psychological punishment by the parent.

The *social interaction* mechanism is less specific as to the exact type of learning involved. It may involve a combination of modeling and reinforcement.[15] This explanation holds that the characteristic social norms involved in the person's interactions with other significant persons shape his attitudes, values, and behavior. Thus what is learned is a series of complex interpersonal relationships. Examples of attempts to use social interaction as a variable can be found in studies of family communication patterns.[16]

Social Structural Constraints

Social structural explanations of socialization emphasize the person's social environment within which learning takes place. Social variables such as social class, sex, and family size are especially important in explaining learning processes and are often useful "control" variables in socialization research. Although they can have a direct or indirect impact on the development of the person's learning properties, the question of their nature of influence (whether direct or indirect) appears to be answerable only through empirical research.[17]

Age or Life-Cycle Position

Although the study of socialization was once restricted to learning that takes place during childhood, it has been extended in recent years to include the study of learning that occurs throughout a person's lifetime.[18] Because people learn continuously and because they learn different things at different times in their lives from different agents, the emphasis is on changes in a person's cognitions and behaviors as he moves through the life cycle, specifically, in the post-adolescent period when persons get married, take a job, and so forth at different ages. Therefore, the term "life cycle" is preferred over "age" as a more relevant variable in adult socialization, because life-styles associated with particular cycles become more crucial in terms of reorganization of various cognitions and behaviors.[19] Thus all generalizations are conditional to a particular phase in the developmental process or life cycle, and a different cluster of variables tends to dominate each stage.

To summarize, the socialization perspective suggests that social roles are acquired through interaction between the person and various agents in specific social settings. The emphasis is on changes in the content or criterion behavior at different ages or stages in the life cycle. All generalizations apply only to a given phase in the person's life cycle, because a different set of variables may be dominant at each stage of the person's development or life cycle.

Although a complete socialization theory must deal with

all types of variables, it is unlikely that any single research study would handle all five types as measured or manipulated variables.[20] Because of the nature of this study, the investigation concentrated on only four of the five variables: content of learning, source of influence, social structural constraints, and age. It did not examine the learning processes. Although the study could suggest potential explanations for learning processes of consumer behavior, a cross-sectional survey did not seem to be the best design for studying such processes.

Consumer Socialization

In line with the general conceptual framework discussed previously, this section deals with variables and hypothesized relationships among these variables specifically dealing with consumer socialization. First, it discusses the concept of consumer role (content or criterion variable). Second, it states hypotheses with respect to the effects of specific agent-adolescent interactions and social structural and maturational factors on the specific consumer-learning cognitions and behaviors that comprise the concept of the consumer role as defined for this study.

Consumer Role

Because so much of this research draws heavily from sociological and psychological theories of socialization, which posit the notion of role acquisition, it seems appropriate to think of consumer behavior in terms of role enactment. This approach may be particularly helpful if one includes in the concept of consumer-role enactment what Ward describes as:

the set of physical and mental activities specially involved in purchase decisions—shopping, talking to others about products and brands and weighing purchase criteria. At such times, skills, knowledge and attitudes directly relevant to the transaction are quite useful.[21]

But consumer role enactment in this research was not confined to purchase decisions. It also included indirectly relevant skills that motivated purchase and consumption, as well as socially desirable behaviors that may contribute to efficient utilization of economic resources for the satisfaction of the maximum number of society's members. Thus "consumer role" is defined in line with Brim's broad concept of the person's "role" in society.[22] Using Brim's definition, the consumer-role concept includes the knowledge, skills, attitudes, predispositions, and subsequent behaviors that make an individual a more *or* less effective consumer in the marketplace.

Ward distinguishes between two types of consumer learning. The first kind includes skills, knowledge, and attitudes that are *directly* relevant to consumption behavior and transaction itself.[23] Examples of directly relevant consumer-learning properties are skills at budgeting and pricing, knowledge of available alternatives, and attitudes toward marketing stimuli, such as advertising and brands. The second kind of consumer learning, according to Ward, involves *indirectly* relevant skills, knowledge, and attitudes, which motivate purchase or consumption but are not directly useful in the purchasing decision or transaction itself. Examples include the many kinds of motivations for consumption (e.g., economic and social motivations) and perceptions of material goods (e.g., materialistic attitudes).[24]

Another scheme classifies the various criteria of consumer learning by levels of cognitive complexity. Gagné's model of cumulative learning, for example, distinguishes between simple and complex learning rules (skills).[25] The first category may include simple definitional statements (definitional and analytical schemata), and the second includes relational statements.

Previous research has used typologies of consumer-learning skills according to levels of cognitive complexity. Blatt and his associates, for example, conceptualized materialism (i.e., orientations emphasizing possessions and money for personal happiness and social progress) and television advertising effects (i.e., influence of commercials on purchase behavior) as complex learning skills.[26] They considered advertising recall (i.e., aided recall of slogans) and attitudes toward television advertising simple learning skills. Similarly, Moore and Stephens conceptualized price accuracy (i.e., ability to price selected products) and brand specification (i.e., comprehension) as complex learning skills; they considered attitudes toward television advertising and slogan recall simple learning skills.[27]

This research focused on the development of specific aspects of consumer-learning properties, commonly referred to as "consumer skills," that may have implications in terms of the issues for consumer socialization research.[28] The specific consumer-learning skills examined are classified on the basis of their cognitive complexity (simple vs. complex) and their relevance to the consumption behavior or transaction (direct vs. indirect). These two dimensions provide a fourfold classification of consumer-learning skills of interest in this research (Table 1).

The first category, *direct-simple*, includes cognitive and affective orientations toward marketing variables—attitudes toward advertisements, salespeople, prices, brands, and stores. The *indirect-simple* skills include knowledge about one's legal rights in the marketplace and knowledge of economic and business concepts. The *direct-complex* skill category includes the ability to filter puffery in advertisements, the ability to cognitively differentiate advertising stimuli, the ability to seek information, and the ability to manage consumer finances. Finally, the *indirect-complex* skill category includes two kinds of predispositions or motives: materialism and consumption (buying) motives. The specific consumption motives examined were economic and social motives.

Explanatory Variables

This study includes two types of explanatory variables: intervening (socialization) processes and environmental variables (social and demographic factors) that locate the adolescent in his social environment. Although social structural constraints and age, in effect, may serve as antecedents of consumer socialization, certain socialization processes, such as frequency of agent-adolescent interaction, and motivations for interaction may intervene to affect the final outcomes of consumer socialization.[29] This notion of consumer learning as a social process contrasts with the view that it is merely a criterion state of knowledge. The mass media, for example, may be seen as agents of socialization rather than simply as dispensers of product information,[30] "because they may serve to shape consumer attitudes and behavior."[31]

Table 1: Classification of Select Cognitive Consumer Skills

Cognitive Complexity

	Simple	Complex
Direct	Responses to Marketing Variables: Attitudes toward advertising Attitudes toward salespeople Attitudes toward prices Attitudes toward brands Attitudes toward stores	Discriminatory Skills: Puffery filtering Cognitive differentiation Information seeking Consumer finance management
Indirect	Consumer Affairs Knowledge: Consumer legislation Economic concepts	Predispositions/Values: Materialism Consumption motivations —Economic —Social

Relevancy to Consumption Behavior (left axis label)

Note: This typology was adapted from previous research. See Joan Blatt et al., "A Cognitive Development Study of Children's Reactions to Television Advertising," in Eli A. Rubinstein et al., eds., *Television and Social Behavior IV—Television in Day to Day Use: Patterns of Use* (Washington, D.C.: U.S. Government Printing Office, 1971); Robert M. Gagné, "Contributions of Learning to Human Development," in John Eliot, ed., *Human Development and Cognitive Processes* (New York: Holt, Rinehart and Winston, Inc., 1971); Roy L. Moore and Lowndes F. Stephens, "Some Communication and Demographic Determinants of Adolescent Consumer Learning," *Journal of Consumer Research*, September 1975; and Scott Ward, "Consumer Socialization," *Journal of Consumer Research*, September 1974.

In line with previous research in consumer socialization,[32] Table 2 classifies the main variables proposed in this research into *antecedents, intervening information processes*, and *outcomes* (consumer skills) that comprise the concept of the consumer role. The variables included are those that are incorporated into specific hypotheses.

Hypotheses

Relationships Between Intervening Processes and Consumer Skills

Previous consumer socialization studies have used the terms "learning processes," "consumer socialization processes," and "intervening information processes" interchangeably to refer to agent-adolescent interaction, without any reference to the specific type of learning that may take place (modeling, reinforcement, or interaction).[33] This study similarly used the terms "intervening information processes" and "socialization processes" to refer to agent-adolescent relationships that may influence consumer skill acquisition.

Table 2: Classification of Main Variables in Proposed Research

Explanatory Variables

Antecedents	Information Sources	Criterion Variables
Social Structural *Constraints* Socioeconomic status Sex *Age*	*Family* (Communication about consumption) *Mass Media* TV exposure time Public affairs media use Social utility for TV ad viewing Social utility for TV program viewing *Peer* (Communication about consumption) *School* (Formal consumer education)	*Individual* (see Table 1) *Social* (Consumer activism)

Specifically, this research examined the influence on adolescent consumers of four socialization agents: *family*, *mass media*, *school*, and *peers*.

Family: As an agent of socialization, the family plays a significant role in influencing how the child acquires his consumer skills. Early sociologists speculated that young people learn basic "rational" aspects of consumption from their parents.[34] Recent research findings appear to support this contention. For example, research by Moore and Stephens shows that overt parent-child communication about consumption predicts fairly well the adolescent's knowledge of prices of selected products.[35] Similarly, Ward and Wackman found that parental "general goals" included teaching their children about price-quality relationships.[36] These findings suggest the following hypotheses:

H1: There is a positive relationship between the frequency of intrafamily communication about consumption and the degree to which the adolescent holds economic motivations for consumption.

H2: There is a positive relationship between the frequency of intrafamily communication about consumption and the strength of the adolescent's attitudes toward prices.

H3: There is a positive relationship between the frequency of intrafamily communication about consumption and the adolescent's ability to manage consumer finances.

Mass Media: The influence from mass media comes mainly from two areas: programming and advertising. Programming may exert some direct or indirect influence on consumer learning. For example, the young person may aspire to have the material blessings of certain television characters.[37] However, of the two, advertising is believed to have the major influence on consumer learning.[38]

Among the best known models of advertising effects (influence) are the "hypodermic" persuasion model, the "limited effects" model, and the "information-seeking" model. The hypodermic persuasion model is a simple learning model based on stimulus-response theories. It predicts that repeated exposure to a message is sufficient to change the attitudes and behaviors of the audience.[39] The limited effects model views the audience as being so active and selective in the communication process that its reaction to the message tends to reinforce existing beliefs rather than change them.[40] Finally, the information-seeking model views the communication process as a two-way street, with the receiver actively involved in the communication process in an effort to solve problems.[41] Parallel to Bauer's notion of an active audience, a "uses and gratifications" model examines the audience's specific motivations for being active in the communication process.[42]

With respect to advertising effects on adolescent consumer learning, previous research suggests that simple consumer-learning skills may be acquired through mere exposure to television—i.e., through repetition. Findings reported by Ward and Wackman, and Keiser, for example, show that accuracy of slogan recall and attitudes toward advertisements are positively related to the amount of television viewing.[43] Similarly, preferences for television programming content may lead to learning of various aspects of consumer learning. For example, it was found that viewing of public affairs programs by adolescents led to greater political knowledge.[44]

On the other hand, mere exposure to the medium may not be sufficient for the learning of complex skills. Because of their nature, complex skills may require information process-ing to be learned, hence more involvement of the viewer with the medium. Research findings reported by Ward and Wackman suggest that complex skills may be acquired as a result of the quality of television advertising (motivation for watching commercials) rather than the quantity of media used (amount of exposure to media).[45]

To summarize, the hypodermic model of communication effects may explain the acquisition of certain (perhaps simple) consumer learning skills, but it may not adequately describe how consumers learn from television advertisements and the TV medium in general.[46] It would also be inaccurate to consider communication as merely a reinforcer of existing cognitive states or behavioral patterns,[47] particularly when socialization processes are characterized by attitude forma-tion and learning.[48] Certain complex consumer skills may be learned as a result of the audience's preference for television and advertising content. Thus the communications effects model for consumer learning should combine exposure to the medium as well as motivations or gratifications sought from the medium. Such a model has recently been referred to as a "transactional model."[4][9]

H4: The amount of television viewing correlates positively with the adolescent's favorability of attitudes toward advertising.[50]

H5: The amount of television viewing correlates positively with the strength of the adolescent's favorable attitudes toward brands.

H6: The amount of television viewing correlates positively with the strength of the adolescent's favorable attitudes toward stores.

H7: The amount of public affairs media use correlates positively with the amount of the adolescent's consumer affairs knowledge.

Bandura considers television commercials to be dispensers of product information and argues that people learn from television advertising through observation and imitation how to attach social meaning to material goods, i.e., the "expressive" or "adaptive" elements of consumption.[51]

> In positive (advertising) appeals, following the recommended action results in a host of rewarded outcomes. Smoking a certain brand of cigarettes or using a particular hair lotion wins the loving admiration of voluptuous belles, enhances job performance, masculinizes one's self-concept, tranquilizes irritable nerves, invites social recognition and amicable responsiveness from total strangers, and arouses affectionate reactions in spouses.[52]

Bandura's speculation about the learning of conspicuous consumption suggests the following hypotheses:

H8: The amount of television viewing correlates positively with the strength of the adolescent's social motivations for consumption.

H9: The amount of television viewing correlates positively with the strength of the adolescent's favorable attitudes toward materialism.

Although Bandura tends to subscribe to the hypodermic

model of communication effects, recent research suggests that learning of social and materialistic orientations about consumption may be a second-order consequence of more fundamental aspects of social learning. For example, one study found no relationship between materialism and exposure to television, but it found significant relationships between materialism and social utility reasons for watching commercials (e.g., watching commercials to form impressions of what kinds of people buy certain brands and to make associations between products and various life-styles).[53] Thus learning also may occur as a function of the quality of television advertising use (gratifications sought in advertisements), which may be conditioned by social interpersonal processes.

H_{10}: Social utility reasons for paying attention to advertisements correlate positively with the strength of the adolescent's attitudes toward materialism.

H_{11}: Social motivations for consumption correlate positively with social utility reasons for paying attention to advertisements.

H_{12}: Social utility reasons for viewing television programs correlate positively with the adolescent's favorable attitudes toward materialism.

H_{13}: Social motivations for consumption correlate positively with social utility reasons for watching television programs.

School: The school is usually charged with the responsibility of "preparing the youth to function as adults by giving them the skill, attitude, and knowledge bases necessary for good citizenship and economic self-sufficiency."[54] Economic competence, for example, is widely accepted as one of the goals of elementary school education, and this is shown in the courses offered. The typical course of study contains activities and topics that might help develop economic understanding. Among the areas of focus of such economic education courses has been the emphasis on knowledge and skills of interest to this study, such as understanding of business terms and practices, some basic vocabulary of economics, intelligent money management, and the ability to select and use goods and services wisely.[55]

Although questions have been raised about the validity of

certain consumer education materials and practices,[56] this study presumes that formal consumer education contributes to the learning of certain consumer skills.

H_{14}: A positive relationship exists in adolescents between the amount of formal consumer education and the amount of consumer affairs knowledge.

Because the school is a social institution reflecting the needs and goals of the society,[57] the following hypothesis is proposed:

H_{15}: A positive relationship exists in adolescents between the amount of formal consumer education and the degree of consumer activism.

Peers: Adolescent peer groups are particularly significant sources of influence.[58]

> The child's ripening need for independence leads him psychologically away from his parents and kin, but, unable to establish a state of personal independence (as in work and marriage) he moves instead into the pseudo-independence of the peer group, where he gains the solace of like situated persons, in the process of substituting a dependence on the peers for his earlier dependence on parents.[59]

Riesman and Roseborough,[60] as well as Parsons and his colleagues,[61] speculated that children learn "expressive elements of consumption" or "affective consumption" ("styles and moods of consumption") from their peers.

H_{16}: The frequency of peer communication about consumption is positively related to the degree of social motivations for consumption held by adolescents.

Effects of Social Structural Constraints

Social structural constraints, such as social class and sex, may affect the acquisition of some consumer learning skills either directly or indirectly. Previous research in the area of adolescent consumer behavior suggests that social structural variables may have a direct impact on adolescent consumer learning. For example, one study found significant differences in responses between white- and blue-collar families with respect to the criteria used to select clothes: white-collar families gave more emphasis to "social" criteria (fit and color), whereas blue-collar families emphasized "functional" or "economic" criteria (durability and warmth).[62] These findings suggest that low-income families may be placing different emphasis on purchasing or evaluative criteria (hence on motivations for consumption) than are high-income families in other types of buying decisions.

H_{17}: The strength of the adolescent's social motivations for consumption is positively related to social class.

H_{18}: The strength of the adolescent's economic motivations for consumption is negatively related to social class.

From a learning theory point of view, Ward argues that because adolescents from low-income homes have less experience with money, and may be less aware of the range of consumer goods, their learning of some aspects of the consumer role should be less adequate than that of adolescents from upper income homes who have more opportunities for consumption.[63] Similarly, Riesman and his associates speculated that in the more affluent families children acquire some understanding of money and purchasing processes at a relatively early age.[64] Williams presents empirical findings that appear to support this line of reasoning.[65] Her research shows that knowledge of economic concepts was greater among children from upper socioeconomic family backgrounds than among children from lower socioeconomic backgrounds. Other studies also report positive relationships between social class and other aspects of the consumer role, such as brand and store preferences[66]; cognitive defenses toward persuasive marketing stimuli, such as attitudes toward salespeople[67] and advertising[68]; consumer affairs knowledge[69]; and information seeking.[70] These findings suggest the following hypotheses:

H_{19}: The strength of the adolescent's favorable attitudes toward brands is positively related to social class.

H_{20}: The strength of the adolescent's favorable attitudes toward stores is positively related to social class.

H_{21}: The strength of the adolescent's favorable attitudes toward salespeople is negatively related to social class.

H_{22}:   The strength of the adolescent's favorable attitudes toward advertising is negatively related to social class.

H_{23}:   The amount of the adolescent's consumer affairs knowledge is positively related to social class.

H_{24}:   The amount of the adolescent's information seeking on products is positively related to social class.

Social structural constraints may also have an indirect effect on adolescent consumer learning. Findings in behavioral science suggest that socialization processes differ according to social structural factors such as socioeconomic status, sex, and birth order.[71] Whether such factors affect consumer socialization processes appears to be purely an empirical question.

Maturational Effects

Theories of cognitive development attempt to explain socialization as a function of qualitative changes (stages) in cognitive organization occurring between infancy and adulthood. Stages are defined in terms of cognitive structures the child can use in perceiving and dealing with the environment at different ages. Thus cognitive-developmental theories stress the interaction of personal and environmental factors.[72]

General assumptions of cognitive-developmental theories include:

1. Basic development involves basic transformations of cognitive *structure* which cannot be defined or explained by the parameters of associationistic learning (contiguity, repetition, reinforcement, etc.), and which must be explained by parameters of organizational wholes or systems of internal relations.

2. Development of cognitive structure is the result of processes of *interaction* between the structure of the organism and the structure of the environment, rather than being the direct result of maturation or the direct result of learning (in the sense of direct shaping of the organism's responses to accord with environmental structures).

3. Cognitive structures are always structures (schemata) of *action*. While cognitive activities

move from the sensorimotor to the symbolic to verbal-propositional modes, the organization of these modes is always an organization of actions upon objects.

4. The direction of development of cognitive structure is toward greater equilibrium in this organism-environment interaction, i.e., of greater balance of *reciprocity* between the action of the (perceived) object upon the organism.[73]

Central to the cognitive-developmental position is the idea of cognitive stages, which are described in Piaget's theory of intellectual development.[74] Stages are described in terms of changes or qualitative differences in cognitive organizations occurring between infancy and adulthood. These changes form an invariant sequence, order, or succession in individual development; and each of these different and sequential modes of thought forms a "structured whole." These cognitive structures are hierarchical integrations, with higher stages displacing the structure found at lower stages.[75]

Little consumer research has been conducted emphasizing cognitive-developmental notions to explain how young people learn consumer behavior. Most published research based on the cognitive-developmental theory is found in the area of people's response to commercials and is limited almost entirely to children.[76]

Although the cognitive-developmental models (e.g., Piaget), which suggest that all socialization occurs by the age of 15, have been widely accepted, some researchers have presented findings suggesting that some kinds of socialization—particularly political—take place after 15 years of age.[77] Therefore, it is no surprise to find evidence, albeit cross-sectional, that consumer learning (and hence consumer socialization) occurs throughout high school.[78] The findings of these investigators suggest that development and integration of some complex consumer skills may be completed during the high school years.

Thus, contrary to the cognitive-developmental theory of socialization (especially Piaget's theory of intellectual development,[79] which suggests that only younger adolescents at the formal operations stage [ages 11 to 15] are still developing and integrating various cognitive skills), this study expects older adolescents to still be developing and integrating complex skills. Thus age differences and integration of complex cognitive skills are expected to be found among younger and older adolescents. No age differences are expected to be found among younger and older adolescents with respect to simple cognitive consumer skills.[80]

H_{25}: Older adolescents (9th through 12th graders) have acquired complex consumer-learning skills to a significantly greater extent than younger adolescents (6th, 7th, and 8th graders).

H_{26}: There are no significant differences in the degree to which older and younger adolescents possess simple consumer-learning skills.

H_{27}: Consumer-learning skills are well integrated (i.e., moderately correlated at fairly high levels of proficiency) among older adolescents but not among younger adolescents.[81]

---

1. D.A. Goslin, ed., *Handbook of Socialization Theory and Research* (Chicago: Rand McNally and Company, 1969); and Scott Ward, "Consumer Socialization," *Journal of Consumer Research*, September 1974, pp. 1-14.

2. Jack M. McLeod and Garret O'Keefe, Jr., "The Socialization Perspective and Communication Behavior," in G. Kline and P. Tichenor, eds., *Current Perspectives in Mass Communication Research* (Beverly Hills, California: Sage Publications, 1972).

3. Orville G. Brim, "Socialization through the Life Cycle," in O. Brim and S. Wheeler, eds., *Socialization After Childhood* (New York: John Wiley & Sons, Inc., 1966), pp. 3-49; Steven H. Chaffee, Jack M. McLeod, and Daniel B. Wackman, "Family Communication Patterns and Adolescent Political Participation," in J. Dennis, ed., *Explorations of Political Socialization* (New York: John Wiley & Sons, Inc., 1972); and Goslin, *Handbook of Socialization Theory and Research*.

4. McLeod and O'Keefe, "The Socialization Perspective and Communication Behavior."

5. Brim, "Socialization through the Life Cycle"; and Paul Secord and Carl W. Backman, *Social Psychology* (New York: McGraw-Hill, 1964).

6. McLeod and O'Keefe, "The Socialization Perspective and Communication Behavior."

7. Ibid., p. 126.

8. Brim, "Socialization through the Life Cycle."

9. McLeod and O'Keefe, "The Socialization Perspective and Communication Behavior."

10. Brim, "Socialization through the Life Cycle."

11. McLeod and O'Keefe, "The Socialization Perspective and Communication Behavior."

12. Steven H. Chaffee, Jack M. McLeod, and Charles K. Atkin, "Parental Influences on Adolescent Media Use," *American Behavioral Scientist*, January-February 1971, pp. 232-240.

13. Ward, "Consumer Socialization."

14. McLeod and O'Keefe, "The Socialization Perspective and Communication Behavior."

15. Ibid.

16. Chaffee, McLeod, and Atkin, "Parental Influences on Adolescent Media Use"; Chaffee, McLeod, and Wackman, "Family Communication Patterns and Adolescent Political Participation"; and Daniel B. Wackman, Jack M. McLeod, and Steven H. Chaffee, "Family Communication Patterns and Cognitive Differentiation," unpublished paper (Madison, Wisconsin: Mass Communication Research Center, University of Wisconsin-Madison, 1970).

17. McLeod and O'Keefe, "The Socialization Perspective and Communication Behavior."

18. Brim, "Socialization through the Life Cycle."

19. McLeod and O'Keefe, "The Socialization Perspective and Communication Behavior."

20. Ibid.

21. Ward, "Consumer Socialization," p. 3.

22. Brim, "Socialization through the Life Cycle."

23. Ward, "Consumer Socialization."

24. Ibid.

25. Robert M. Gagné, "Contributions of Learning to Human Development," in John Eliot, ed., *Human Development and Cognitive Processes* (New York: Holt, Rinehart, and Winston, Inc., 1971), pp. 111-128.

26. Joan Blatt, Lyle Spencer, and Scott Ward, "A Cognitive Development Study of Children's Reactions to Television Advertising," in Eli A. Rubinstein, George H. Comstock, and John P. Murray, ed., *Television and Social Behavior, IV—Television in Day to Day Use: Patterns of Use* (Washington, D.C.: U.S. Government Printing Office, 1971).

27. Roy L. Moore and Lowndes F. Stephens, "Some Communication and Demographic Determinants of Adolescent Consumer Learning," *Journal of Consumer Research*, September 1975, pp. 80-92.

28. Thomas S. Robertson, "The Impact of Television Advertising on Children," *Wharton Quarterly*, Summer 1972; and Ward, "Consumer Socialization."

29. Moore and Stephens, "Some Communication and Demographic Determinants of Adolescent Consumer Learning"; and Scott Ward and Daniel B. Wackman, "Family and Media Influences on Adolescent Consumer Learning," *American Behavioral Scientist*, January-February 1971, pp. 415-427.

30. Ibid.

31. Moore and Stephens, "Some Communication and Demographic Determinants of Adolescent Consumer Learning," p. 81.

32. Moore and Stephens, "Some Communication and Demographic Determinants of Adolescent Consumer Learning"; and Ward, "Consumer Socialization."

33. Moore and Stephens, "Some Communication and Demographic Determinants of Adolescent Consumer Learning"; and Ward and Wackman, "Family and Media Influences on Adolescent Consumer Learning."

34. T. Parsons, R.F. Bales, and E.A. Shils, *Working Papers in the Theory of Action* (Glencoe, Illinois: The Free Press, 1953); and David Riesman and Howard Roseborough, "Careers and Consumer Behavior," in Lincoln Clark, ed., Consumer Behavior Vol. II, *The Life Cycle and Consumer Behavior* (New York: New York University Press, 1955).

35. Moore and Stephens, "Some Communication and Demographic Determinants of Adolescent Consumer Learning."

36. Scott Ward and Daniel B. Wackman, "Effects of Television Advertising on Consumer Socialization," Working Paper (Cambridge, Massachusetts: Marketing Science Institute, 1973).

37. Arthur M. Vener and Charles R. Hoffer, *Adolescent Orientation to Clothing* (East Lansing, Michigan: Agricultural Experiment Station, Michigan State University, 1959).

38. Robertson, "The Impact of Television Advertising on Children."

39. A parallel thesis to the hypodermic model is the low-commitment view of advertising effects. Both models assume that media exposure equals audience effect. See, for example, Jack M. McLeod and Lee B. Becker, "Testing the Validity of Media Gratifications through Political Effects Analysis," in J.G. Blumler and E. Katz, eds., *The Uses of Mass Communication* (Beverly Hills, California: Sage Publications, 1974); Michael L. Rothschild, "Involvement as a Determinant of Decision Making Styles," *Proceedings* (Chicago: American Marketing Association, 1975), pp. 216-220; and Thomas S. Robertson, "Low-Commitment Consumer Behavior," *Journal of Advertising Research*, April 1976, pp. 19-24.

40. Joseph T. Klapper, *The Effects of Mass Communication* (New York: Free Press, 1960).

41. Raymond A. Bauer, "The Obstinate Audience: The Influence Process from the Point of View of Social Communication," *American Psychologist*, May 1964, pp. 319-328.

42. Elihu Katz, Jay G. Blumler, and Michael Gurevitch, "Utilization of Mass Communication by the Individual," in Jay G. Blumler and Elihu Katz, eds., *The Uses of Mass Communication* (Beverly Hills, California: Sage Publications, 1974).

43. Stephen K. Keiser, "Awareness of Brands and Slogans," *Journal of Advertising Research*, August 1975, pp. 37-43; and Ward and Wackman, "Family and Media Influences on Adolescent Consumer Learning."

44. Chaffee, McLeod, and Wackman, "Family Communication Patterns and Adolescent Political Participation."

45. Ward and Wackman, "Family and Media Influences on Adolescent Consumer Learning."

46. R.B. Zajonc, "Attitudinal Effects of Mere Exposure," *Journal of Personality and Social Psychology Monograph Supplement*, 1968.

47. Klapper, *The Effects of Mass Communication*.

48. Ward and Wackman, "Family and Media Influences on Adolescent Consumer Learning."

49. McLeod and Becker, "Testing the Validity of Media Gratifications through Political Effects Analysis."

50. This hypothesis was based on empirical findings presented by Glen W. Thompson, "Children's Acceptance of Television Advertising and the Relation of Television to School Achievement," *Journal of Educational Research*, December 1964, pp. 171-174.

51. Albert Bandura, "Modeling Influences on Children," Testimony to the Federal Trade Commission, November 1971. Similar speculations regarding the learning of "expressive" or "adaptive" elements of consumption were made by Parsons, Bales, and Shils, *Working Papers in the Theory of Action*, as well as by Riesman and Roseborough, "Careers in Consumer Behavior."

52. Ward, "Consumer Socialization," p. 7.

53. Ward and Wackman, "Family and Media Influences on Adolescent Consumer Learning."

54. Earnest Q. Campbell, "Adolescent Socialization," in David A. Goslin, ed., *Handbook of Socialization Theory and Research* (Chicago: Rand McNally, 1969), p. 844.

55. Ruth W. Gavian and Louis C. Nanassy, "Economic Competence as a Goal of Elementary School Education," *Elementary School Journal*, January 1955, pp. 270-273.

56. See, for example, S.L. Diamond, "Consumer Education: Perspectives on the State of the Art," unpublished paper (Washington, D.C., Howard University, Graduate School of Business Administration, 1974); and Ward, "Consumer Socialization."

57. Brim, "Socialization through the Life Cycle."

58. See, for example, Campbell, "Adolescent Socialization"; and Paul Gilkison, "Teen-agers' Perceptions of Buying Frame of Reference: A Decade of Retrospect," *Journal of Retailing*, Summer 1973, pp. 25-37.

59. Campbell, "Adolescent Socialization," p. 824.

60. Riesman and Roseborough, "Careers and Consumer Behavior."

61. Parsons, Bales, and Shils, *Working Papers in the Theory of Action.*

62. North Central Research Committee NC-24, *Adolescent Girls' Skirts. Part I: Mothers' and Daughters' Opinions of School Skirts*, Station Bulletin 478, NCR Research Pub-169 (St. Paul: Agricultural Experiment Station, University of Minnesota, 1965).

63. Ward, "Consumer Socialization."

64. David Riesman, Nathan Glazer, and Renel Denny, *The Lonely Crowd* (New Haven: Yale University Press, 1950).

65. Joyce W. Williams, "A Gradient of the Economic Concepts of Elementary School Children and Factors Associated with Cognition," *Journal of Consumer Affairs*, Summer 1970, pp. 113-123.

66. Lester P. Guest, "The Genesis of Brand Awareness," *Journal of Applied Psychology*, December 1942, pp. 800-808.

67. Philip R. Cateora, *An Analysis of the Teen-age Market* (Austin, Texas: Bureau of Business Research, University of Texas, 1963).

68. Scott Ward and Thomas S. Robertson, "Adolescent Attitudes toward Television Advertising: Preliminary Findings," paper presented to the American Marketing Association Convention, September 1970.

69. Thomas D. Horn and Lebery Miller, "Children's Concepts Regarding Debt," *Elementary School Journal*, March 1955, pp. 406-412.

70. Scott Ward, Daniel B. Wackman, and Ellen Wartella, *Children Learning to Buy: The Development of Consumer Information Processing Skills*, Report No. 75-120 (Cambridge, Massachusetts: Marketing Science Institute, November 1975).

71. R.D. Hess, "Social Class and Ethnic Influences on Socialization," in Paul H. Mussey, ed., *Manual of Child Psychology*, Vol. 2, 3rd ed. (New York: John Wiley & Sons, Inc., 1970), pp. 457-459.

72. Lawrence Kohlberg, "The Cognitive Developmental Approach to Socialization," in D.A. Goslin, ed., *Handbook of Socialization Theory and Research* (Chicago: Rand McNally and Co., 1969).

73. Ibid., p. 348.

74. Jean Piaget, "The General Problems of the Psychological Development of the Child," in J.M. Tanner and B. Elders, eds., *Discussions on Child Development: Proceedings of the World Health Organization Study Group on the Psychological Development of the Child: IV* (New York: International Universities Press, 1960).

75. Kohlberg, "The Cognitive Developmental Approach to Socialization," pp. 352-353.

76. Ward, "Consumer Socialization."

77. Kent M. Jennings and Richard G. Niemi, "Patterns of Political Learning," *Harvard Educational Review*, Summer 1968, pp. 443-467.

78. See, for example, Horn and Miller, "Children's Concepts Regarding Debt"; Keiser, "Awareness of Brands and Slogans"; Bernice M. Moore and Way H. Holzman, *Tomorrow's Parents: A Study of Youth and Their Families* (Austin, Texas: University of Texas Press, 1965); Moore and Stephens, "Some Communication and Demographic Determinants of Adolescent Consumer Learning"; and Ward and Wackman, "Family and Media Influences on Adolescent Consumer Learning."

79. Herbert Ginsburg and Sylvia Opper, *Piaget's Theory of Intellectual Development* (Englewood Cliffs, New Jersey: Prentice-Hall, 1969).

80. These speculations are along similar lines of reasoning found in Moore and Stephens, "Some Communication and Demographic Determinants of Adolescent Consumer Learning."

81. For a more elaborate discussion of the rationale of this hypothesis, see Moore and Stephens, "Some Communication and Demographic Determinants of Adolescent Consumer Learning."

Chapter 3

Methodology

Sample

The sample for this study consisted of 806 adolescent students from 13 schools in 7 geographical areas in Wisconsin. Some of the schools within each geographical area were chosen on a convenience basis; others were chosen on a random basis. Table 3 lists the cities and towns from which samples were selected, the schools that participated, the number of subjects from each school who completed questionnaires, the number of usable questionnaires obtained, and the number of usable questionnaires chosen for the final analysis of this study.

The investigator contacted school officials to ask for their cooperation and delivered questionnaires to those who agreed to cooperate. Most of the questionnaires were mailed; therefore, the researcher had little control over the types of classes in which they were completed. Regular class sessions were used for filling in the questionnaires, and most students needed 30 to 45 minutes to complete the 10-page questionnaire (see Appendix A). The questionnaires were administered to classes by teachers.

Most of the classes chosen by school officials to participate in the survey were consumer-related courses such as home

Table 3: Breakdown of Total Sample by Participating School

Town/City	School	Completed Questionnaires	Usable Questionnaires	Subjects Used in Analysis*
Stoughton	Stoughton Middle	110	96	43
	Stoughton High	80	65	55
Necedah	Necedah Middle	108	94	74
	Necedah High	40	25	25
Verona	Verona Middle	83	70	49
	Verona High	129	81	66
Appleton	Appleton Middle†	71	64	57
	Appleton High†	175	166	158
Janesville	Janesville Middle	96	67	60
Oregon	Oregon High	176	138	90
Sun Prairie	Sun Prairie Junior	46	39	0††
Poynette	Poynette Middle	333	286	129
	Poynette High	30	25	0††
Total		1,477	1,216	806

*The number of subjects used in the final analysis is not equal to the number of usable questionnaires because of the sampling that was done from the usable number of questionnaires in each school (see discussion at the end of "sample" section).
†Denotes that data was collected from two different schools.
††No subjects were used in the final analysis because the sample served as a pretest.

economics and consumer education. Because of this, some subsamples contained a disproportional representation of the sexes. Table 4 shows that 525 females and 281 males made up the sample, meaning that nearly two-thirds of the respondents were female.

All age groups were fairly well represented, as is shown in Table 5. The average age was approximately 14 years and 9 months, a fairly accurate representation of the average period of adolescence (12 to 18 years). The final sample consisted of 441 younger adolescents (under 15 years) and 365 older adolescents (15 years and over) (Table 5).

The sample reflected a cross-section of various population density regions and socioeconomic backgrounds. Appleton is an urban area of approximately 130,000 inhabitants located in the eastern portion of the state of Wisconsin, approximately 100 miles north of Milwaukee. Janesville, an urban area of approximately 50,000 residents, is located in the southern part of the state approximately 50 miles southeast of Madison and 70 miles southwest of Milwaukee. Blue-collar

Table 4: Percentage of Male and Female Respondents in Participating Schools

School	Males		Females		Total Number of Respondents
Stoughton Middle	25	(58.1%)	18	(41.9%)	43
Stoughton High	14	(25.5%)	41	(74.5%)	55
Necedah Middle	31	(41.9%)	43	(58.1%)	74
Necedah High	0	(00.0%)	25	(100.0%)	25
Verona Middle	24	(49.0%)	25	(51.0%)	49
Verona High	23	(34.8%)	43	(65.2%)	66
Appleton Middle	0	(00.0%)	57	(100.0%)	57
Appleton High	62	(39.2%)	96	(60.8%)	158
Janesville Middle	0	(00.0%)	60	(100.0%)	60
Oregon High	32	(35.6%)	58	(64.4%)	90
Poynette Middle	70	(54.3%)	59	(45.7%)	129
Total	281	(34.9%)	525	(65.1%)	806

factory workers make up a large portion of the Janesville population. Verona, Stoughton, and Oregon are suburban areas located within 15 miles south of Madison, a city with 170,000 residents. Oregon and Verona each have about 2,500 inhabitants, and Stoughton's population exceeds 6,000. People from many different socioeconomic backgrounds live in all three towns. Poynette and Necedah are mainly rural farming communities of approximately 1,000 and 700 residents, respectively. Poynette is located about 30 miles north of Madison, and Necedah is in the middle of the state approximately 100 miles east of LaCrosse and northwest of Madison.

Table 5: Age Distribution of Respondents

Age Range	Number of Respondents	Percentage of Respondents
Under 12	7	.90
12 to 13	58	7.20
13 to 14	147	18.24
14 to 15	229	28.41
15 to 16	107	13.27
16 to 17	62	7.69
17 to 18	97	12.03
18 to 19	97	12.03
Over 19	2	.23
Total	806	100.00

Table 6 shows mean values and standard deviations of the respondent's socioeconomic characteristics measured by Duncan's SES index using a two-digit occupational percentile code.[1] (The higher the number is, the higher is the socioeconomic status of the respondent. Values range from 0 to 96.) Data in Table 6 show that respondents were a fairly accurate representation of the socioeconomic characteristics of residents in their respective areas.

Thus, although logistics prevented random selection of subjects, the sample was fairly representative of respondents of various demographic and socioeconomic characteristics. This was facilitated by drawing subsamples from the usable number of questionnaires in each school and trying to balance out the characteristics of subjects included in the final sample.

Definition and Measurement of Variables

Criterion Variables

Consumer-role measures were taken in the following areas: (1) responses to marketing stimuli; (2) consumer affairs knowledge; (3) discriminatory skills; (4) predisposition/values; and (5) consumer activism.

Table 6: Mean Values and Standard Deviation of Respondents' Socioeconomic Status in Each School Using Duncan's SES Index

School	Mean Value	Standard Deviation
Stoughton Middle	42.38	24.10
Stoughton High	43.25	25.53
Necedah Middle	34.27	21.96
Necedah High	34.97	25.87
Verona Middle	48.55	24.70
Verona High	51.13	22.30
Appleton Middle	50.81	26.10
Appleton High	39.02	24.43
Janesville Middle	25.94	17.27
Oregon High	42.20	23.33
Poynette Middle	35.27	23.68
Average Total	40.11	24.41

• *Response to marketing stimuli* by adolescents was considered a simple consumer-learning skill directly related to consumption or transaction. This category includes attitudes toward advertising, salespeople, prices, brands, and stores.

General attitudes toward advertising was operationally defined as a construct of cognitive and affective orientations concerning liking of and belief in advertising; efficacy and purpose of advertising; interest in advertising; and liking of advertising in various media.[2] This variable was measured by summing responses to the following items:

Most television commercials are fun to watch.

When I see or hear something new advertised, I often want to buy it.

Advertisements help people buy things that are best for them.

Most radio commercials are annoying. (Reverse score)

I think there should be less advertising than there is now. (Reverse score)

Most advertising that comes through the mail is junk and not worth looking at. (Reverse score)

Most magazine advertisements are enjoyable to look at.

Most advertisements tell the truth.

I don't pay much attention to advertising. (Reverse score)

Most newspaper advertisements are enjoyable to look at.

Responses were measured on a 5-point "strongly agree-strongly disagree" Likert-type scale. The reliability of this scale was .54 as measured by coefficient alpha. (Reliability of a measure refers to the extent to which the results obtained from it are repeatable. The reliability of the scales used in this research were estimated by coefficient alpha. Reliabilities of above .50 are sufficient for constructs in the early stages of research.[3])

General attitudes toward salespeople was operationally defined as a construct of affective and cognitive orientations concerning the integrity, friendliness, and politeness of salespeople and belief in and helpfulness of salespeople. This variable was measured by summing responses to the following items:

Most salespeople try to trick you into buying something you don't really need. (Reverse score)

Salespeople are honest.

Salespeople are friendly.

Most salespeople would take advantage of those who don't know much about buying things. (Reverse score)

Salespeople are polite.

Responses were measured on a 5-point "strongly agree-strongly disagree" Likert-type scale. This variable had a coefficient alpha reliability of .56.

Attitudes toward prices was operationally defined as a construct of cognitive and affective orientations toward price-product relationships concerning prices as indicators of product quality and performance. This variable was measured by summing responses to the following items:

Many products are not worth the price you pay for them. (Reverse score)

Most products sold at reduced price are of poor quality. (Reverse score)

Most products sold at reduced price are never really on sale at all. (Reverse score)

Most products are sold at reduced prices because they are too old. (Reverse score)

Responses to these items were similarly measured on a 5-point "strongly agree-strongly disagree" Likert scale. The alpha reliability coefficient of this scale was fairly low (.28).

Attitudes toward brands was operationally defined as a construct of affective and cognitive orientations toward familiar brand names of products and brand names as indicators of product quality and performance. This variable was measured by summing responses to the following items:

Advertised brands are better than those not advertised.

Quality products are made by well-known companies.

I prefer a certain brand of most products I buy or use.

I don't care about the brand names of most products I buy. (Reverse score)

Brand-name products work better than "off-brands."

Responses to these items were measured on a 5-point "strongly agree-strongly disagree" Likert-type scale. The coefficient alpha for this scale was .50.

Attitudes toward stores was operationally defined as affective orientations toward stores and cognitive orientations concerning the name of the store as an indicator of product quality and performance. Measurement was made by summing responses to the following items:

Once I have made a choice on which store to buy things from, I prefer shopping there without trying other stores.

Well-known stores never sell poor quality products.

I prefer doing most of my shopping in the same stores I have always shopped in.

I judge the value of some products by the name of the store that sells them.

Responses to these items were measured on a 5-point "strongly agree-strongly disagree" Likert-type scale. The reliability coefficient alpha of the attitudes-toward-stores scale was .52. The items designed to measure respondents' attitudes toward advertising, salespeople, prices, brands, and stores were not presented together but were dispersed throughout the scale (see Appendix A).

• The adolescent's *knowledge of consumer affairs* is considered a simple learning skill indirectly relevant to consumption. For the purpose of this study, the concept comprises two specific consumer affairs knowledge variables: knowledge of economic and business concepts and knowledge of consumer-related legislation.

Knowledge of economic concepts referred to the accuracy of cognitions held with respect to basic terms in the following areas: economics, banking, finance, insurance, real estate, and marketing.[4] *Knowledge of consumer legislation* refers to cognitions held with respect to unit pricing, bait advertising, code dating, and remedies available to consumers.[5] Measurement of the variable was made by summing responses representing *correct* answers to the following items:

When you buy stock you own part of a company.

Milk sold in the store must show the last date it can be sold.

A "shortage economy" is when the country is short of money.

The mortgage is the down payment on a house.

When you have liability insurance you don't have to pay for wrecking someone else's car.

The Better Business Bureau helps consumers, not merchants.

A credit union is a group of people who agree to save their money together and make loans to each other.

Ground beef sold at the store must have two prices: one that shows how much the whole package costs and another that says how much one pound costs.

All products show the name of the company that makes them.

It is legal for a store to advertise a product at $20.00 and sell it for $21.00 on the same day.

The Office of Consumer Protection helps people who have been tricked by merchants.

Respondents were asked to indicate whether they thought each of these items was *True*, *False*, or *Don't Know*. Thus the accuracy index would range from 0 to 11, depending upon the number of correct responses. The alpha reliability coefficient of this scale was .57.

• *Discriminatory skills* are considered complex skills directly relevant to consumption. This category includes puffery filtering, cognitive differentiation of advertising, information seeking, and consumer finance management.

Puffery filtering referred to the respondent's ability to discriminate "facts" from exaggeration in advertising. This variable was an accuracy index of "completely true-partly true-not true at all" advertising claims. Puffery items were adapted from previous studies[6] and 40 judges were used to determine the degree of puffery in each item. The final list consisted of twelve items. Six of these items were considered (on the basis of the pretest) to contain the greatest amount of puffery; the other six were considered to contain "true" information. The items were the following:

Chevrolet's engine guarantee is for 60,000 miles or 5 years. (True)

State Farm is all you need to know about insurance. (Puffery)

Honda Civic gets 43 miles per gallon on the highway. (True)

Arm & Arm—the first spray deodorant with baking soda. (True)

The American breakfast, no mistake, starts with sugar, milk, and Kellogg's corn flakes. (Puffery)

Amana—the greatest cooking discovery since fire. (Puffery)
Bayer works wonders. (Puffery)
Sanka is 97% caffeine-free coffee. (True)
Mr. Coffee—the fastest American coffee maker. (True)
Brylcream makes success go to your head. (Puffery)
Presto cooks a hamburger in 60 seconds. (True)
Ultra Brite can help your love life. (Puffery)

Responses were measured on a 3-point scale. Respondents were given scores of 1, 2, and 3 for checking puffery items as "believe it is completely true," "believe it is partly true," and "believe it is not true at all," respectively; and scores of 3, 2, and 1 for providing similar responses to advertising claims considered to be true. The accuracy index could range from 12 to 36. The alpha reliability coefficient was .25.

Cognitive differentiation was operationally defined as the ability to identify products that are claimed to be different on specific attributes.[7] This variable was measured by asking respondents to write the names of twelve products or brands selected at random from a larger group of items of relevance to adolescents that were observed advertised during prime-time programs over a 3-month period and summing up items to form a 0- to 12-point index, which had a reliability coefficient of .86. The twelve items were the following:

_____makes 0 to 50 miles in 8.2 seconds.

_____is more effective in helping stop wetness than any leading brand.

_____penetrates deeper than most nasal sprays.

_____TV has the best picture and fewer repairs.

_____camera weighs 16 ounces and costs $66.00.

_____, the candy mint with retsyn.

_____, the TV network of the Olympic games.

_____, the natural pH balance shampoo.

_____, the astronauts' drink.

_____, the toothpaste with baking soda.

_____, the soap with cocoa butter and moisturizers.

When you catch a cold you take one _____ capsule every twelve hours.

Information seeking was operationally defined as an expressed need to consult various information sources prior to purchase.[8] Measurement of the extent of information seeking was made by summing the number of sources the adolescent might rely on for information or advice prior to purchasing a camera, hair dryer, pocket calculator, bicycle, or a wrist watch. Alternative information sources were "friends," "TV ads," "salespersons," "consumer reports," "one or both of my parents," and "newspaper or magazine ads." These products were selected on the basis of previous studies,[9] relevance to adolescents' consumer behavior, and amount of socioeconomic and performance risk. Previous researchers have used this approach and suggested its desirability.[10] The alpha reliability coefficient was .37.

Consumer finance management referred to the ability to correctly price selected expense items of an average family's monthly budget. Respondents were asked to estimate about how much the average American family with two children and a total monthly income of $1,000 spends on each of the following items: food, clothes, home expenses, automobile expenses, other expenses, and savings. Respondents were assigned a score of 5 for responses falling approximately within plus or minus ten percent of the actual expense item estimates, a 4 for responses falling within plus or minus twenty percent of the actual figures, 3 for responses falling within plus or minus thirty percent, a 2 for responses falling within plus or minus forty percent, and a score of 1 for responses falling approximately within plus or minus fifty or more percent of the actual estimates. The actual estimates for the expense items were obtained from the U.S. Department of Labor.[11] The accuracy index could range from 6 to 30. The alpha reliability coefficient was .61.

• Two types of variables relevant to consumer predispositions are materialism and consumption motivation.

Materialism was operationally defined in this research as an "orientation emphasizing possession and money for personal happiness and social progress."[12] It was measured by soliciting responses to six items, many of which are similar to Ward and Wackman.[13]

It is really true that money can buy happiness.

My dream in life is to be able to own expensive things.

People judge others by the things they own.

I buy some things that I secretly hope will impress other people.

Money is the most important thing to consider in choosing a job.

I think others judge me as a person by the kinds of products and brands I use.

Responses to these items were measured on a 5-point "strongly agree-strongly disagree" Likert-type scale. This scale had a reliability coefficient alpha of .60.

Economic motivations for consumption were operationally defined as cognitive orientations concerning the importance of product functional and economic features, orientation toward comparison shopping, and significant discriminating attributes.[14] This variable was measured on a 0- to 25-point index by summing responses to consumption situations possessing various degrees of such properties. Respondents were asked to check whether they thought it was important to know five different items before buying a bicycle, watch, camera, pocket calculator, or hair dryer, as follows:

Guarantees on different brands.

Name of the company that makes the product.

Whether any brands are on sale.

Kinds of materials different brands are made of.

Quality of store selling a particular brand.

Responses were summed across each item to form a 0- to 5-point index for each item. Thus scores could range from 0 to 25. The reliability of this five-item scale (coefficient alpha) was .69.

Social motivations for consumption were operationally defined as a construct of cognitive orientations concerning the importance of conspicuous consumption and self-expression via conspicuous consumption.[15] Measurement was made on a 0- to 20-point index by summing responses to consumption situations of various degrees of social visibility.

Respondents were asked to indicate whether they thought it was important to know four different items before buying a bicycle, watch, camera, pocket calculator, or hair dryer:

What friends think of different brands or products.

What kinds of people buy certain brands or products.

What others think of people who use certain brands or products.

What brands or products to buy to make good impressions on others.

Responses were summed across each item to form a 0- to 5-point index representing the number of products for which the respondent had checked each item. Scores could range from 0-20. The coefficient alpha of this four-item scale was .85.

● *Consumer Activism.* It is assumed that socially desirable consumer behaviors are those contributing to the economic system's efficient functioning and utilization of economic resources producing satisfaction for the maximum number of people. An effective buyer is assumed to be the person who can meet the specified demands of the society. Such demands may include (a) income allocation according to tastes and preferences for goods, (b) use of available information, and (c) rational decision making in the marketplace.[16]

An effective consumer, on the other hand, is a person who uses products in a rational and efficient way, usually referred to as "responsible consumption." Such social demands may include efficient use of products and resources with respect to global human population.[17]

Consumer activism was measured by summing responses to the following seven items developed in line with those used in previous research.[18]

I keep track of the money I spend and save.

I plan how to spend my money.

I shop around before buying something that costs a lot of money.

I carefully read *most* of the things they write on packages or labels.

I compare prices and brands before buying something that costs a lot of money.

I try to buy returnable bottles instead of disposable ones.

I make sure that the lights and TV set at home are off when they are not being used.

Responses to these items were measured on a 5-point "Quite a lot-Don't know" scale. The alpha reliability coefficient of this scale was .64.

Explanatory Variables

Two kinds of measures of explanatory variables were obtained: (1) measures related to the adolescent's interaction with the socialization agents and (2) measures of antecedent variables. The first measure consisted of items designed to tap the adolescent's frequency of interaction with each of the four socialization agents: (1) parents, (2) mass media, (3) peers, and (4) school.

Family: One variable was relevant in this research with respect to the adolescent's frequency of interaction with family members. *Family communication about consumption* was defined as overt interaction between parent and adolescent (both positive and negative) concerning goods and services.[19] It was measured by summing responses to the following items:

My parents tell me what things I should or shouldn't buy.

My parents want to know what I do with my money.

I help my parents buy things for the family.

My parents complain when they don't like something I bought for myself.

My parents ask me what I think about things they buy for themselves.

My parents and I talk about things we see or hear advertised.

I ask my parents for advice about buying things.

My parents tell me why they buy some things for themselves.

I go shopping with my parents.

My parents tell me I should decide about things I should or shouldn't buy.

My parents and I talk about buying things.

My parents tell me what they do with their money.

Responses to these items were measured on a 5-point "Very often-Never" Likert-type scale. The reliability coefficient alpha was .64.

Mass Media: Adolescent mass media measures included (a) amount of television viewing, (b) public affairs media use, (c) social utility reasons for watching television advertisements, and (d) social utility reasons for watching television programs.

Amount of *television viewing* was measured by asking respondents how frequently they watched specific program categories.[20] Responses to program content were measured on a 5-point "Every day-Never" scale and summed to form the television viewing index. (Responses were solicited to the following categories: national and local news, sport events, movies, variety shows, cartoons, police and adventure shows, comedy shows.) The index could range from 7 to 35. Previous studies used this approach of measuring the amount of television viewing and suggested its desirability.[21] The alpha reliability coefficient of this scale was .67.

Public affairs media use referred to national and local TV news viewership as well as frequency of reading the following items in the newspaper: news about the government and politics, news about the economy, and advertisements. (The index was constructed by summing items measured on a 5-point "Every day-Never" scale.[22]) The index could range from 4 to 20. The alpha reliability coefficient of this scale was .66.

Social utility reasons for watching television advertisements were operationally defined as motivations to watch television commercials as a means of gathering information about life-styles and behaviors associated with uses of specific consumer products.[23]

Measurement was made by summing responses to the following items indicating social utility reasons for viewing television commercials:

To get ideas on how to be successful.

To find out what kinds of people use certain products.

To find out what kinds of products to buy to feel like those people I wish I were.

To learn what things to buy to make good impressions on others.

To dream of the good life.

To find out what qualities people like in others.

To find out how others solve the same problems I have.

To give me something to talk about with others.

To learn about the "in" things to buy.

To tell others something they don't already know about new ideas or products.

Positive responses were summed to form a 0- to 10-point scale. The coefficient alpha for the total scale was .64.

Social utility reasons for watching television programs were operationally defined as motivations to watch television shows as a means of gathering information about life-styles and behaviors associated with uses of specific products. Measurement was made by summing responses to items similar to those used in measuring the previous variable. The coefficient alpha of this scale was .70.

Peers: One variable was relevant in this research with respect to the adolescent's interaction with his peers. *Peer communication about consumption* was operationally defined as overt peer-adolescent interactions concerning goods and services. This variable was measured by summing responses to the following items:

I ask my friends for advice about buying things.
My friends and I talk about buying things.
My friends and I talk about things we see or hear advertised.
My friends ask me for advice about buying things.
My friends tell me what things I should or shouldn't buy.
I go shopping with my friends.

Responses to these items were measured on a 5-point "Very often-Never" Likert-type scale. The reliability coefficient alpha for this scale was .78.

School: Learning at school may take place through such mechanisms as reinforcement (grades), interaction (informal discussion of the subject matter with other students), and perhaps through modeling (e.g., unconscious identification with teachers).[24] Thus a major difficulty arises in analyzing a school as a socialization agent because it may be functioning as a separate social system by itself. *Formal consumer education* in this research refers to the number of consumer-related courses taken in school. Students were asked to state the "number of courses they have taken" in each of the following areas: consumer education, home economics, economics, environmental sciences, and guidance (job education). They were also asked to write the names of any other courses in which they had studied about consumer matters. Number of courses taken in all areas was summed to form a single index.

Socioeconomic status was measured using Duncan's SES index.[25] Respondents were asked to state their father's and mother's occupations and place of work. Open-ended responses for father's occupation were used to construct the social-class measure. Previous socialization studies used this approach and suggested its desirability.[26]

Information on the respondent's *sex* was obtained by asking the subjects to check whether they were "male" or "female." Responses were coded as 1 for male and 2 for female.

Age was used as a discrete variable to classify adolescents into younger adolescents (under 15) and older adolescents (15 and over), in line with Piaget's theory.[27]

---

1. Otis D. Duncan, "A Socioeconomic Index of All Occupations," in Albert J. Reiss, Jr., ed., *Occupations and Social Status* (New York: Free Press, 1961).

2. Don L. James, *Youth, Media, and Advertising* (Austin, Texas: Bureau of Business Research, University of Texas, 1971); John R. Rossiter and Thomas S. Robertson, "Children's TV Commercials: Testing for Defenses," *Journal of Communication*, Autumn 1974, pp. 137-144; Glen W. Thompson, "Children's Acceptance of Television Advertising and the Relation of Television to School Achievement," *Journal of Educational Research*, December 1964, pp. 171-174; and Scott Ward and Daniel Wackman, "Family and Media Influences on Adolescent Consumer Learning," *American Behavioral Scientist*, January-February 1971, pp. 415-427.

3. For a discussion of coefficient alpha, see J.C. Nunnally, *Psychometric Theory* (New York: McGraw-Hill Book Company, 1967).

4. Ruth W. Gavian and Louis C. Nannassy, "Economic Competence as a Goal of Elementary School Education," *Elementary School Journal*, January 1955, pp. 270-273; and Joyce W. Williams, "A Gradient of the Economic Concepts of Elementary School Children and Factors Associated with Cognition," *Journal of Consumer Affairs*, Summer 1970, pp. 113-123.

5. Gavian and Nannassy, "Economic Competence as a Goal of Elementary School Education"; and Eric Schnapper, "Consumer Legislation and the Poor," *The Yale Law Journal*, 1971, pp. 745-768.

6. Ivan L. Preston and Ralph Johnson, "Puffery—A Problem FTC Didn't Want (and May Try to Eliminate)," *Journalism Quarterly*, Autumn 1972, pp. 558-568.

7. See the discussion by Daniel B. Wackman, Jack M. McLeod, and Steven H. Chaffee, "Family Communication Patterns and Cognitive Differentiation," unpublished paper (Madison, Wisconsin: Mass Communication Research Center, University of Wisconsin-Madison, 1970); and R.B. Zajonc, "The Process of Cognitive Tuning in Communication," *Journal of Abnormal and Social Psychology*, September 1960, pp. 159-167.

8. Roy L. Moore and Lowndes F. Stephens, "Some Communication and Demographic Determinants of Adolescent Consumer Learning," *Journal of Consumer Research*, September 1975, pp. 80-92.

9. Paul Gilkison, "Teen-agers' Perceptions of Buying Frame of Reference: A Decade of Retrospect," *Journal of Retailing*, Summer 1973, pp. 25-37; and Moore and Stephens, "Some Communication and Demographic Determinants of Adolescent Consumer Learning."

10. Moore and Stephens, "Some Communication and Demographic Determinants of Adolescent Consumer Learning."

11. U.S. Bureau of Labor Statistics, *Monthly Labor Review*, July 1974, p. 39.

12. Ward and Wackman, "Family and Media Influences on Adolescent Consumer Learning," p. 426.

13. Ibid.

14. Raymond A. Bauer, "The Obstinate Audience: The Influence Process from the Point of View of Social Communication," *American Psychologist*, May 1964, pp. 319-328.

15. Ibid.; and Scott Ward and David G. Gibson, "Social Influence and Consumer Uses of Information," paper submitted to Advertising Division, Association for Education in Journalism, Berkeley, California, August 1969.

16. Schnapper, "Consumer Legislation and the Poor."

17. George Fisk, "Criteria for a Theory of Responsible Consumption," *Journal of Marketing*, January 1973, pp. 24-31.

18. Gavian and Nannassy, "Economic Competence as a Goal of Elementary School Education"; and Schnapper, "Consumer Legislation and the Poor."

19. Moore and Stephens, "Some Communication and Demographic Determinants of Adolescent Consumer Learning"; and Ward and Wackman, "Family and Media Influences on Adolescent Consumer Learning."

20. Jack M. McLeod and Garret J. O'Keefe, Jr., "The Socialization Perspective and Communication Behavior," in G. Kline and P. Tichenor, eds., *Current Perspectives in Mass Communication Research* (Beverly Hills, California: Sage Publications, 1972).

21. Steven H. Chaffee, Jack M. McLeod, and Charles K. Atkin, "Parental Influences on Adolescent Media Use," *American Behavioral Scientist*, January-February 1971, pp. 323-340; and McLeod and O'Keefe, "The Socialization Perspective and Communication Behavior."

22. Jack M. McLeod and Lee B. Becker, "Testing the Validity of Media Gratifications Through Political Effects Analysis," in Jay G. Blumler and Elihu E. Katz, eds., *The Uses of Mass Communications* (Beverly Hills, California: Sage Publications, 1974).

23. Moore and Stephens, "Some Communication and Demographic Determinants of Adolescent Consumer Learning"; and Ward and Wackman, "Family and Media Influences on Adolescent Consumer Learning."

24. Earnest Q. Campbell, "Adolescent Socialization," in David A. Goslin, ed., *Handbook of Socialization Theory and Research* (Chicago: Rand McNally, 1969).

25. Duncan, "A Socioeconomic Index for All Occupations."

26. Moore and Stephens, "Some Communication and Demographic Determinants of Adolescent Consumer Learning"; and Ward and Wackman, "Family and Media Influences on Adolescent Consumer Learning."

27. Herbert Ginsburg and Sylvia Opper, *Piaget's Theory of Intellectual Development* (Englewood Cliffs, New Jersey: Prentice-Hall, Inc., 1969).

Chapter 4

Analyses and Results

This chapter presents the results of statistical analyses that were performed to test the specific hypotheses stated in Chapter 2. The two main types of analyses discussed are: (1) analyses that were performed to examine the effects of antecedent variables on the various consumer skills and (2) analyses regarding the test of the specific hypotheses in this research.

Important Antecedents of Adolescent Consumer Learning

Sex

Table 7 shows mean values of the dependent variables for male and female adolescents. Significant differences emerged between the two groups of seven of the fourteen dependent variables. Male adolescents had more favorable attitudes toward stores, greater consumer affairs knowledge, greater materialistic values, and stronger social motivations for consumption than female adolescents. Female adolescents, on the other hand, showed more favorable attitudes toward advertising, were more able to differentiate advertising stimuli, and scored significantly higher on the information-seeking measure than did their male counterparts.

Table 7: Mean Values of Dependent Variables for Male and Female Adolescents

Dependent Variables	Male Adolescents (N = 281)		Female Adolescents (N = 525)		t-value
Attitudes toward advertising	23.68	(5.59)	27.77	(5.32)	7.36†
Attitudes toward brands	14.20	(3.23)	14.36	(3.27)	.45
Attitudes toward stores	11.40	(2.79)	10.44	(2.78)	10.38††
Attitudes toward prices	10.60	(2.60)	10.62	(2.51)	.01
Attitudes toward salespeople	17.07	(3.50)	16.71	(3.52)	1.96
Consumer affairs knowledge	6.19	(2.00)	5.75	(1.80)	10.16††
Cognitive differentiation	5.72	(2.56)	6.39	(2.20)	14.95††
Puffery filtering	28.08	(2.49)	28.25	(2.40)	.93
Consumer finance management	15.45	(4.58)	15.86	(4.62)	1.43
Information seeking	11.11	(5.19)	11.83	(4.68)	4.10*
Materialism	18.23	(4.53)	16.72	(4.06)	23.29††
Social motivations	6.66	(4.31)	5.78	(4.33)	7.51†
Economic motivations	15.56	(5.92)	15.18	(6.03)	1.96
Consumer activism	23.94	(3.35)	24.26	(3.34)	1.73

*Significant at .05 level.
†Significant at .01 level.
††Significant at .001 level.
Note: Table entries are mean values for each group. Standard deviations are in parentheses.

Social Class

Significant differences were found between the lower and middle social classes—the two main social groups represented—in only five consumer-learning skills: consumer affairs knowledge, cognitive differentiation, puffery filtering, consumer finance management, and economic motivations for consumption (Table 8). It was found that middle-class adolescents possessed these skills to a significantly greater degree than did lower class adolescents.

Age

Several significant differences emerged between the younger and older adolescents (Table 9). Younger adolescents had significantly more favorable attitudes toward advertising, brands, and prices than older adolescents. Older adolescents, on the other hand, scored higher than younger adolescents on the following consumer-skill measures: consumer affairs knowledge, cognitive differentiation,

Table 8: Mean Values of Dependent Variables for Lower Class and Middle Class Adolescents

Dependent Variables	Lower Class (N = 563)		Middle Class (N = 243)		t-value
Attitudes toward advertising	27.54	(5.34)	27.04	(5.65)	1.43
Attitudes toward brands	14.42	(3.36)	14.04	(2.99)	2.41
Attitudes toward stores	10.64	(2.75)	10.72	(2.92)	.14
Attitudes toward prices	10.56	(2.56)	10.73	(2.49)	.73
Attitudes toward salespeople	16.70	(3.46)	17.14	(3.62)	2.66
Consumer affairs knowledge	5.79	(1.86)	6.16	(1.92)	6.43*
Cognitive differentiation	6.01	(2.34)	6.49	(2.35)	6.96*
Puffery filtering	28.05	(2.43)	28.51	(2.40)	6.13*
Consumer finance management	15.33	(4.60)	16.60	(4.50)	13.09†
Information seeking	11.43	(4.87)	11.92	(4.88)	1.70
Materialism	17.17	(4.19)	17.44	(4.51)	.69
Social motivations	6.13	(4.20)	6.00	(4.65)	.16
Economic motivations	15.61	(6.03)	16.81	(5.83)	6.86†
Consumer activism	24.06	(3.33)	24.36	(3.38)	1.37

*Significant at .01 level.
†Significant at .001 level.
Note: Table entries are mean values for each group. Standard deviations are in parentheses.

Table 9: Mean Values of Dependent Variables for Younger and Older Adolescents

Dependent Variables	Younger Adolescents (N = 441)		Older Adolescents (N = 365)		t-value
Attitudes toward advertising	28.13	(5.39)	26.50	(5.36)	18.22††
Attitudes toward brands	14.58	(3.26)	13.95	(3.22)	6.79†
Attitudes toward stores	10.54	(2.82)	10.82	(2.78)	2.03
Attitudes toward prices	10.91	(2.67)	10.25	(2.33)	13.61††
Attitudes toward salespeople	16.88	(1.75)	16.77	(1.76)	.22
Consumer affairs knowledge	5.37	(1.82)	6.54	(1.76)	83.70††
Cognitive differentiation	5.84	(2.23)	6.53	(2.44)	17.24††
Puffery filtering	28.03	(2.43)	28.39	(2.43)	4.54*
Consumer finance management	15.41	(4.69)	16.07	(4.92)	4.10*
Information seeking	11.17	(4.63)	12.07	(5.12)	6.88†
Materialism	17.27	(4.18)	17.22	(4.41)	.02
Social motivations	5.99	(4.26)	6.21	(4.44)	.53
Economic motivations	15.56	(5.96)	16.46	(6.02)	4.52*
Consumer activism	23.80	(3.25)	24.56	(3.25)	10.45††

*Significant at .05 level.
†Significant at .01 level.
††Significant at .001 level.
Note: Table entries are mean values for each group. Standard deviations are in parentheses.

puffery filtering, consumer finance management, information seeking, economic motivations for consumption, and consumer activism.

The Independent Effects

To investigate the independent effects of each of these factors, a three-way analysis of variance was performed with eight possible treatment groups defined by sex(2) x age(2) x SES(2). Table 10 shows mean values of the dependent variables for each treatment group; F-ratios highlighting the significant main and interaction effects are shown in Table 11.

When the effects of sex and age were controlled, middle-class adolescents were found to possess greater consumer affairs knowledge; they were better able to estimate the average family's monthly expenditures on major classes of products; and they had stronger economic motivations for consumption than their lower class counterparts.

When the effects of sex and social class were taken into account, significant age differences emerged for half of the variables examined. Specifically, older adolescents had greater amounts of consumer affairs knowledge; they were better able to cognitively differentiate product attribute information in advertisements, manage consumer finances, and seek information from a variety of sources prior to decision making; and they were more likely to perform "socially desirable consumer behaviors" than their younger counterparts. Younger adolescents, on the other hand, had more favorable attitudes toward advertising and prices than older adolescents. These findings suggest that with increasing age adolescents tend to (1) develop greater resistance to persuasive advertising, (2) understand better marketing strategies relating to the pricing of products, and (3) generally become more sophisticated consumers. The results may further suggest the development of general discontent toward marketing stimuli and practices as young people acquire more experience with the marketplace.

The final concern in this research was the impact of sex differences on adolescent consumer behavior. Table 10 shows mean values of the dependent variable for male and female adolescents of various socioeconomic and age characteristics.

Table 10: Values for Dependent Variables by Treatment Group

Independent Variables:

	Male				Female			
Sex								
Age	Younger		Older		Younger		Older	
Social Class	Lower	Middle	Lower	Middle	Lower	Middle	Lower	Middle
Dependent Variables:								
Attitudes toward advertising	28.04	26.17	25.87	25.42	28.71	27.65	26.50	28.87
	(5.35)	(6.28)	(5.38)	(5.44)	(5.04)	(5.71)	(5.33)	(5.18)
Attitudes toward brands	14.75	13.77	14.18	13.35	14.71	14.38	13.94	14.25
	(3.47)	(3.13)	(2.97)	(3.0)	(3.31)	(2.84)	(3.49)	(3.03)
Attitudes toward stores	10.91	11.23	11.33	11.02	10.35	10.19	10.48	10.83
	(2.73)	(3.34)	(2.54)	(2.91)	(2.69)	(2.95)	(2.90)	(2.64)
Attitudes toward prices	10.89	10.70	10.18	10.59	10.88	11.13	10.11	10.43
	(2.88)	(2.57)	(2.37)	(2.28)	(2.55)	(2.77)	(2.36)	(2.24)
Attitudes toward salespeople	16.85	17.24	17.18	17.23	16.79	17.01	16.21	17.16
	(3.59)	(3.29)	(3.43)	(3.65)	(3.48)	(3.66)	(3.34)	(3.78)
Consumer affairs knowledge	5.44	5.61	6.93	7.08	5.27	5.46	6.14	6.57
	(1.91)	(2.06)	(1.69)	(1.87)	(1.74)	(1.80)	(1.75)	(1.65)
Cognitive differentiation	5.31	5.26	6.29	6.04	5.95	6.58	6.44	6.29
	(2.54)	(2.41)	(2.56)	(2.57)	(2.02)	(2.00)	(2.39)	(2.23)
Puffery filtering	27.77	28.10	28.06	28.79	27.88	28.73	28.48	28.32
	(2.59)	(2.40)	(2.41)	(2.36)	(2.35)	(2.34)	(2.41)	(2.47)
Consumer finance management	14.67	15.26	15.50	17.29	15.39	16.59	15.62	16.86
	(4.69)	(3.82)	(4.48)	(4.69)	(4.71)	(4.85)	(4.46)	(4.26)
Information seeking	10.72	10.59	11.19	11.29	11.26	11.33	11.70	13.14
	(4.89)	(4.99)	(5.48)	(4.97)	(4.34)	(4.50)	(4.91)	(4.71)
Materialism	18.34	16.97	18.14	19.17	16.97	16.75	16.09	17.31
	(4.49)	(4.57)	(4.42)	(4.48)	(3.92)	(3.98)	(3.90)	(4.69)
Social motivations	6.74	7.20	7.08	7.06	5.99	5.56	6.17	5.95
	(4.05)	(5.06)	(4.37)	(5.28)	(4.38)	(4.64)	(4.62)	(4.50)
Economic motivations	14.56	15.44	15.99	17.21	15.41	17.41	16.40	16.64
	(5.68)	(6.22)	(5.95)	(5.86)	(6.08)	(5.53)	(6.18)	(5.91)
Consumer activism	27.31	28.13	28.63	28.81	28.20	17.41	28.73	16.64
	(3.55)	(3.51)	(4.01)	(3.22)	(3.51)	(3.73)	(3.79)	(3.63)
Number of observations	110	39	84	48	213	79	156	77

Note: Table entries are mean scores. Standard deviations are in parentheses.

Table 11: Effects of Independent Variables on Dependent Consumer Skill Measures

Dependent Variables	Main Effects						Interaction Effects
	SES	Age	Sex	SES x Age	SES x Sex	Age x Sex	SES x Age x Sex
Attitudes toward advertising	1.346	8.108*	9.195*	4.947*	3.038	.295	.341
Attitudes toward brands	3.039	3.273	1.379	.580	2.888	.005	.222
Attitudes toward stores	.048	1.194	8.588*	.018	.039	.380	1.621
Attitudes toward prices	.933	7.974*	.050	.680	.180	.624	.401
Attitudes toward salespeople	2.018	.009	1.358	.116	.417	.441	.877
Consumer affairs knowledge	2.737	73.941*	7.999*	.144	.245	2.846	.215
Cognitive differentiation	2.536	15.767*	20.532*	.001	5.745*	.609	.308
Puffery filtering	5.063*	2.252	.775	.591	.224	1.004	3.241
Consumer finance management	10.656*	5.177*	1.395	.704	.002	2.577	.637
Information seeking	.927	4.942*	5.572*	1.079	.997	.490	.549
Materialism	.238	.539	16.396*	7.929*	.971	2.891	.482
Social motivations	.021	.285	9.204*	.037	.577	.064	.230
Economic motivations	5.048*	3.145	1.905	.533	.005	2.400	1.192
Consumer activism	1.083	8.168*	1.038	.088	.436	.305	.620

*Significant at .05 level.
Note: Entries are F-values.

Significant differences between the two groups emerged for half of the dependent variables (Table 11). Male adolescents had more favorable attitudes toward stores, greater consumer affairs knowledge, greater materialistic values, and stronger social motivations for consumption than female adolescents. Female adolescents, on the other hand, showed more favorable attitudes toward advertising and scored significantly higher on the information seeking and cognitive differentiation measures than did their male counterparts.

Three significant interaction effects were found (Table 11). First, the interaction of sex with age appears to affect the adolescent's attitudes toward advertising. The cell means of the scores on this variable are graphically shown in Exhibit 1. The findings suggest that although female teen-agers are more likely to hold favorable attitudes toward advertising than their male counterparts, they also are more likely to experience a greater negative change in these attitudes during adolescence.

Second, there was a significant interaction between sex and social class with regard to the child's ability to discriminate cognitively and retain advertising information; females are better able to do so. Further, although this ability remains fairly stable for males across social class, middle-class females are better able to cognitively differentiate and retain information from television commercials than their lower social class counterparts (Exhibit 2).

The third interaction concerned the combined effects of age and social class on the respondent's materialistic values (Exhibit 3). Although the two variables by themselves appear to have little influence on teen-agers' materialistic orientations, Exhibit 3 shows that with increasing age lower class teen-agers are likely to develop less favorable materialistic attitudes; youths from middle classes are likely to develop stronger materialistic orientations.

Influence of Consumer Socialization Agents

Before testing the hypothesized relationships between sources of information of consumer learning and the various consumer skills (Hypotheses 1 through 16), the investigator took into account the effects of the three antecedent variables (sex, social class, and age). Those antecedent variables

Exhibit 1: Cell Means of Attitudes Toward Advertising Measure

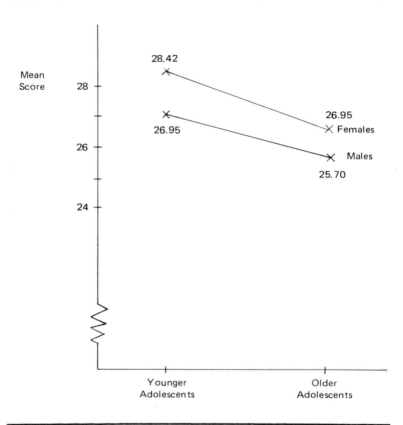

that were found to be significantly related to the dependent variables were included in the analysis as "control" variables.[1]

In testing the hypothesized relationships between sources of information of consumer learning and the dependent variables, simple product-moment correlations were computed. Whenever more than one independent variable was expected or found to be related to a given dependent variable, the effects of such other variables had to be removed. Under those circumstances partial correlation coefficients were computed showing the separate effects of each independent variable on the given dependent consumer skill.

Exhibit 2: Cell Means of Cognitive Differentiation Measure

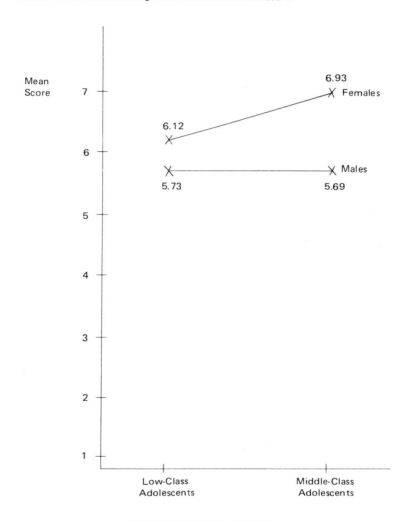

Family

On the basis of sociological theories and some recent empirical findings in the area of consumer learning, it was hypothesized that overt parent-to-adolescent communication

Exhibit 3: Cell Means of Materialism Measure

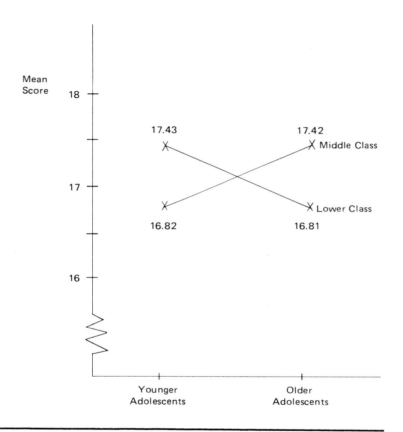

about consumption would correlate positively with the adolescent's economic motivations for consumption (Hypothesis 1), favorability of attitudes toward prices (Hypothesis 2), and ability to manage consumer finances (Hypothesis 3).

Table 12 shows zero-order and partial correlations between parent-adolescent communication about consumption and adolescent's economic motivations for consumption. The resulting correlation coefficient of .082 was large enough to support the first hypothesis (p < .020). This statistically significant relationship also remained after removing the

Table 12: Relationships Between Economic Motivations for Consumption and Selected Explanatory Variables

Independent Variables	Economic Motivations for Consumption	Significance Level
Family communication about consumption	.094 (.082)	.007
Social class	.119 (.119)	.001
Age	.107 (.119)	.002

Note: Table entries are partial correlation coefficients. Zero-order correlations are shown in parentheses.

effects of SES and age that were found to be associated with the level of the adolescents' economic motivations for consumption (Tables 8 and 9). In fact, the resulting partial correlation coefficient for the hypothesized relationship increased slightly (r = .094, p < .007). Thus Hypothesis 1 was fully supported.

In examining the relationship between intrafamily communication about consumption and the adolescent's favorability of attitudes toward prices, the resulting correlation coefficient, which is shown in Table 13, was negative and insignificant (r = −.035, p < .323). The correlation between the two variables changed very little after introducing age into the analysis, since the partial correlation remained negative and was not statistically significant (r = −.045, p < .206). Thus the data did not support Hypothesis 2. These findings, however, should be regarded as tentative because of the low reliability of the construct "attitudes toward prices" (coefficient alpha = .28).

Table 13: Relationships Between Favorability of Attitudes Toward Prices and Selected Explanatory Variables

Independent Variables	Attitudes Toward Prices	Significance Level
Family communication about consumption	−.045 (−.035)	.206
Age	−.090 (−.086)	.011

Note: Table entries are partial correlation coefficients. Zero-order correlations are shown in parentheses.

The last hypothesis with respect to the influence of family on adolescent consumer learning concerned the child's ability to manage a typical family budget. This skill was expressed in terms of the accuracy of pricing of specific expense items for an average family's budget. The data presented in Table 14 do not support Hypothesis 3. Both zero-order and partial correlations between intrafamily communication about consumption and consumer finance management are nearly zero.

These findings suggest that the family may be an important socialization agent in teaching adolescents the economic aspects of purchasing processes and consumption. But it does not seem to shape these young people's attitudes toward prices in general, nor does it provide them with skills for managing consumer finances.

Mass Media

The transactional model of communication effects suggested two sets of hypotheses with respect to the effects of mass media on adolescent consumer learning. The first set of hypotheses concerned the learning of select *simple* cognitive consumer skills; the second set concerned the learning of select *complex* cognitive consumer skills (Table 1).

Simple Consumer Skills: Previous research findings suggested that the learning of some simple consumer skills may merely be a matter of the *amount* and *content* of mass media used by the adolescent. Specifically, it was hypothesized that the amount of television viewing would be correlated positively

---

Table 14: Relationships Between Consumer Finance Management and Selected Explanatory Variables

Independent Variables	Consumer Finance Management	Significance Level
Family communication about consumption	.019 (.001)	.601
Social class	.097 (.125)	.006
Age	.107 (.131)	.002

Note: Table entries are partial correlation coefficients. Zero-order correlations are shown in parentheses.

with the adolescent's favorability of attitudes toward advertising (Hypothesis 4), brands (Hypothesis 5), and stores (Hypothesis 6). It was further hypothesized that the specific content of mass media use—i.e., the amount of public affairs media use—would correlate with the adolescent's amount of consumer affairs knowledge (Hypothesis 7).

The resulting correlation coefficient between *amount* of television viewing and strength of favorable attitudes toward advertising was .192 (p < .001). This correlation was reduced to .160 (but still remained significant at the same level) when age and sex were introduced into the analysis as control variables (Table 15). Thus Hypothesis 4 was adequately supported.

The correlation between amount of television viewing and favorability of attitudes toward brands was equally strong (r = .159, p < .001), offering support for Hypothesis 5. The significant relationship remained when age was introduced into the analysis as a significant control variable. The resulting partial correlation coefficient was .134 (p < .001) (Table 16).

Table 15: Relationships Between Favorability of Attitudes Toward Advertising and Selected Explanatory Variables

Independent Variables	Attitudes Toward Advertising	Significance Level
Amount of television viewing	.160 (.111)	.001
Sex	−.097 (.095)	.006
Age	−.098 (−.155)	.006

Note: Table entries are partial correlation coefficients. Zero-order correlations are shown in parentheses.

Table 16: Relationships Between Favorability of Attitudes Toward Brands and Selected Explanatory Variables

Independent Variables	Attitudes Toward Brands	Significance Level
Amount of television viewing	.134 (.159)	.002
Age	−.046 (−.096)	.192

Note: Table entries are partial correlation coefficients. Zero-order correlations are shown in parentheses.

The amount of television viewing, on the other hand, was not related to the adolescent's favorability of attitudes toward stores. The correlation between the two variables was very low (r = .024, p < .492). This low relationship did not change significantly when controlling for sex (Table 17). Thus Hypothesis 6 was not confirmed.

With respect to the specific *content* of public affairs the adolescent is exposed to in the mass media, the analysis revealed a strong relationship between the amount of public affairs media use and the amount of consumer affairs knowledge (r = .31, p < .001). However, the correlation between the two variables was reduced to .228 when the effects of other variables that were hypothesized or were found to be associated with consumer affairs knowledge were held constant (Table 18). Thus Hypothesis 7 was supported.

Complex Consumer Skills: Sociological theories suggest that adolescents may learn two complex consumer skills from the mass media (television in particular): i.e., materialistic atti-

Table 17: Relationships Between Favorability of Attitudes Toward Stores and Selected Explanatory Variables

Independent Variables	Attitudes Toward Stores	Significance Level
Amount of television viewing	.038 (.024)	.278
Sex	−.110 (−.113)	.001

Note: Table entries are partial correlation coefficients. Zero-order correlations are shown in parentheses.

Table 18: Relationships Between Consumer Affairs Knowledge and Selected Explanatory Variables

Independent Variables	Consumer Affairs Knowledge	Significance Level
Public affairs media use	.228 (.310)	.001
Consumer-related courses	.007 (.055)	.848
Sex	−.079 (−.112)	.025
Social class	.014 (.053)	.689
Age	.340 (.397)	.001

Note: Table entries are partial correlation coefficients. Zero-order correlations are shown in parentheses.

tudes and social motivations for consumption. With respect to the learning processes of these two skills, it was speculated that learning may only partially be a matter of a stimulus-response phenomenon occurring simply as a function of the amount of television viewing. It may also be a function of the quality of media use (gratifications sought in the media, especially social utility reasons). Thus it was hypothesized that the amount of television viewing by the adolescent would positively correlate to the strength of social motivations for consumption (Hypothesis 8) and the favorability of attitudes toward materialism (Hypothesis 9). It also was hypothesized that attitudes toward materialism would be positively related to the adolescent's social utility reasons for watching television commercials (Hypothesis 10) and television programs (Hypothesis 12); and social motivations for consumption were expected to be positively related to social utility reasons for watching television commercials (Hypothesis 11) and to social utility reasons for watching television programs (Hypothesis 13).

A positive statistical relationship ($r = .147$, $p < .001$) was found between the amount of television viewing and the strength of social motivations for consumption. The correlation between the two variables was reduced ($r = .079$, $p < .025$) when the effects of other independent variables were held constant (Table 19). These data provided support for Hypothesis 8.

Table 19: Relationships Between Social Motivations for Consumption and Selected Explanatory Variables

Independent Variables	Social Motivations for Consumption		Significance Level
Amount of television viewing	.079	(.147)	.025
Peer communication about consumption	.127	(.142)	.001
Social utility reasons for watching TV shows	.038	(.154)	−.277
Social utility reasons for watching TV ads	.121	(.194)	.001
Social class	.007	(−.008)	.845
Sex	−.129	(−.096)	.001

Note: Table entries are partial correlation coefficients. Zero-order coefficients are shown in parentheses.

Although the zero-order correlation between social motivations for consumption and social utility reasons for watching television programs is statistically significant, the partial correlation between the two variables is not strong enough (r = .038, p < .277) to support Hypothesis 13 (Table 19). However, the partial correlation between social motivations for consumption and social utility reasons for watching television commercials is statistically significant (r = .121, p < .001) and supports Hypothesis 11. These results suggest that the learning of social motivations for consumption may not only be a function of the adolescent's frequency of interaction with (exposure to) television but also a function of the child's motivations for watching television commercials.

Somewhat similar results emerged about the learning of materialistic attitudes. Although the zero-order correlation between the strength of favorable attitudes toward materialism and the amount of television viewing was statistically significant (r = .134, p < .001), the partial correlation between the two variables was not strong enough to support Hypothesis 9 (Table 20). However, the significant relationships between materialism and social utility reasons for watching television programs (r = .085, p < .016) on the one hand, and between materialism and social utility reasons for watching television commercials (r = .135, p < .001) on the other hand, support Hypotheses 10 and 12, respectively. These findings suggest that the learning of materialistic attitudes may not be a function of the adolescent's mere exposure to television; rather, the learning of these cognitive orientations may develop as a result of the adolescent's social utility motivations for television viewing.

Table 20: Relationships Between Materialism and Selected Explanatory Variables

Independent Variables	Materialism		Significance Level
Amount of television viewing	.054	(.134)	.127
Social utility reasons for watching TV shows	.085	(.179)	.016
Social utility reasons for watching TV ads	.135	(.207)	.001
Sex	−.195	(−.168)	.001

Note: Table entries are partial correlation coefficients. Zero-order correlations are shown in parentheses.

To summarize the effects of mass media on adolescent consumer learning, the amount of television viewing correlated positively with the strength of favorable attitudes toward advertising and brands, but it did not correlate with favorable attitudes toward stores. A strong positive relationship was found between the amount of consumer affairs knowledge and the extent to which the respondents attended to public affairs items in the mass media. Finally, the strength of social motivations for consumption was correlated positively with both the amount of television viewing and the social utility reasons for watching television advertisements; the strength of materialistic attitudes was positively correlated with social utility reasons for watching both television advertisements and shows.

School

Adolescent consumer education at school was hypothesized to correlate positively with the child's consumer affairs knowledge (Hypothesis 14) and to a degree with his consumer activism (Hypothesis 15). Because age was found to be related with both the amount of consumer affairs knowledge and the number of consumer-related courses, it was included in the analysis as a control variable.

Neither the zero-order correlation of .055 nor the partial correlation of .007 between consumer affairs knowledge and formal consumer education was statistically significant, indicating that the data do not support Hypothesis 14 (Table 21). Similarly, the correlation between consumer activism

Table 21: Relationships Between Consumer Affairs Knowledge and Formal Consumer Education, With the Effects of Other Explanatory Variables Removed

Independent Variables	Consumer Affairs Knowledge		Significance Level
Consumer-related courses	.007	(.055)	.848
Public affairs media use	.228	(.310)	.001
Sex	−.079	(−.112)	.025
Social class	.014	(.053)	.689
Age	.340	(.397)	.001

Note: Table entries are partial correlation coefficients. Zero-order correlations are shown in parentheses.

and formal consumer education was .053 (p < .135), and the partial correlation between the two variables was equally small and insignificant (r = .035, p < .323) (Table 22). These small measures of association between the adolescent's consumer education at school and the degree of his consumer activism offer no support for Hypothesis 15.

Because the formal consumer-education measure was constructed by summing the number of consumer-related courses the respondent had taken at school (the average number of such courses for the sample was 3.33), the assessment of the effects of formal consumer education may be difficult. Different courses may emphasize different aspects of consumer behavior. Thus it seemed appropriate to analyze the influence of formal consumer education at school in terms of each *type* of consumer-related course.

Table 23 shows relationships between the amount of consumer affairs knowledge and the number of courses respondents had taken in six different types of consumer-related courses. The resulting correlations between the number of courses taken in each one of the six different consumer-related areas and the amount of the adolescent's consumer affairs knowledge were very low and not statistically significant, suggesting that consumer affairs knowledge may be acquired not only from consumer-related courses at school.

The influence of the various types of consumer-related courses on adolescents' socially desirable consumer behaviors also appears to be insignificant (Table 24). When the effects of age were removed, only courses taken in environmental sciences were significantly related (r = −.082, p < .021) to consumer activism, but the relationship was negative. Thus adolescents who tend to take courses in environmental sciences are *least* likely to engage in effective consumer behaviors.

Table 22: Relationships Between Consumer Activism and Selected Explanatory Variables

Independent Variables	Consumer Activism	Significance Level
Formal consumer education	.035 (.053)	.323
Age	.142 (.148)	.001

Note: Table entries are partial correlation coefficients. Zero-order coefficients are shown in parentheses.

Table 23: Relationships Between Amount of Consumer Affairs Knowledge and Number of Courses Taken in Various Consumer-related Areas, Controlling for Age

Independent Variables	Consumer Affairs Knowledge		Significance Level
Consumer education	.005	(.211)	.879
Home economics	.034	(.028)	.324
Economics	.022	(.048)	.532
Environmental science	−.047	(−.111)	.186
Guidance (job education)	.013	(.079)	.714
Other courses*	.021	(.028)	.548
Age	.253	(.397)	.001

*Includes those courses in which students studied about consumer matters.
Note: Table entries are partial correlation coefficients. Zero-order coefficients are shown in parentheses.

Table 24: Relationships Between Consumer Activism and Number of Courses Taken in Various Consumer-related Areas, Controlling for Age

Independent Variables	Consumer Activism		Significance Level
Consumer education	−.011	(.109)	.761
Home economics	.034	(.083)	.343
Economics	.001	(.047)	.972
Environmental science	−.082	(−.081)	.021
Guidance (job education)	.018	(.042)	.607
Other courses*	−.035	(−.026)	.330
Age	.081	(.148)	.023

*Includes courses in which students studied about consumer-related matters.
Note: Table entries are partial correlation coefficients. Zero-order correlations are shown in parentheses.

Peers

On the basis of sociological theories it was speculated that adolescents may learn "expressive elements of consumption" from peers. Thus it was hypothesized that the frequency of the adolescent's communication with his peers would correlate positively with his degree of social motivations for consumption.

The resulting correlation between the two variables was .142 (p < .001), and the partial correlation was .127 (p < .001) (Table 25). Thus the data appear to support Hypothesis 16, which suggests that adolescents acquire social motivations for consumption from their peers.

Table 25: Relationships Between Social Motivations for Consumption and Peer Communication About Consumption, With the Effects of Other Explanatory Variables Removed

Independent Variables	Social Motivations for Consumption		Significance Level
Peer communication about consumption	.127	(.142)	.001
Amount of television viewing	.079	(.147)	.025
Social utility reasons for watching television shows	.038	(.154)	.277
Social utility reasons for watching television advertisements	.121	(.194)	.001
Social class	.007	(−.008)	.845
Sex	−.129	(−.096)	.001

Note: Table entries are partial correlation coefficients. Zero-order correlations are shown in parentheses.

Social Class Influences on Adolescent Consumer Learning

Another concern of this research was the investigation of the direct effects of social class on adolescent consumer learning. Two sets of hypotheses were formulated with respect to such effects. The first set dealt with the consumer learning of various motivations for consumption. It was hypothesized that social motivations for consumption would be positively related to social class (Hypothesis 17) and that economic motivations for consumption would be negatively related to social class (Hypothesis 18).

The relationship between the adolescent's social class and his social motivations for consumption was not significant (r = −.008, p < .820), even when the effects of other explanatory variables were held constant (r = .007, p < .845) (Table 26). These low measures of association between the two variables did not support Hypothesis 17. Similarly, the data did not support Hypothesis 18. The correlation between social class and economic motivations for consumption was significant (r = .119, p < .001) but in the opposite direction (Table 12), suggesting that adolescents from upper social classes are more likely to possess such consumption motives than are their lower class counterparts.

A second set of hypotheses pertaining to the effects of social class on adolescent consumer learning was formulated on the basis of learning theory, sociological theories, and some empirical findings. It was hypothesized that social class would be positively correlated with the favorability of attitudes toward brands (Hypothesis 19) and stores (Hypothesis 20), amount of consumer affairs knowledge (Hypothesis 23), and amount of product information seeking (Hypothesis 24); it would be negatively correlated with the favorability of attitudes toward salespeople (Hypothesis 21) and advertising (Hypothesis 22).

Table 27 shows relationships between social class and select cognitive consumer skills relating to the foregoing hypotheses. The data support Hypotheses 22 and 24. Thus the higher the adolescent's socioeconomic background the more likely he is to seek information prior to decision making ($r = .085$, $p < .015$) and the least likely he is to have positive attitudes toward advertising ($r = -.080$, $p < .033$). No other hypothesis was supported. The relationship between social class and attitudes toward brands (Hypothesis 19) was statistically significant but in the opposite direction of that hypothesized ($r = -.87$, $p < .014$), suggesting that upper class adolescents are less likely to have favorable attitudes toward brands than lower class adolescents. Similarly,

Table 26: Relationships Between Social Motivations for Consumption and Social Class, With the Effects of Other Explanatory Variables Removed

Independent Variables	Social Motivations for Consumption		Significance Level
Social class	.007	(−.008)	.845
Amount of television viewing	.079	(.147)	.025
Peer communication about consumption	.127	(.142)	.001
Social utility reasons for watching television shows	.038	(.154)	.277
Social utility reasons for watching television advertisements	.121	(.194)	.001
Sex	−.129	(−.096)	.001

Note: Table entries are partial correlation coefficients. Zero-order correlations are shown in parentheses.

Table 27: Relationships Between Social Class and Select Cognitive Consumer Skills

Consumer Skills	Social Class		Significance Level
Attitudes toward:			
Brands	−.087	(O)	.014
Stores	−.038	(O)	.280
Salespeople	.053	(O)	.131
Advertising	−.080	(E)	.023
Consumer affairs knowledge	.053	(E)	.129
Information seeking	.085	(E)	.016

O = Nature of relationship is in the *opposite* direction from that hypothesized.
E = Nature of relationship is in the *expected* direction.
Note: Table entries are zero-order correlations.

the relationships between attitudes toward stores, salespeople, and social class were in the opposite direction and not statistically significant; the correlation between social class and consumer affairs knowledge was in the predicted direction but was not strong enough to support Hypothesis 23.

Maturational Effects

Three hypotheses were formulated on the basis of adolescent cognitive development. First, it was hypothesized that older adolescents would have acquired complex consumer-learning skills to a significantly greater extent than younger adolescents (Hypothesis 25). Second, it was hypothesized that there would be no significant differences among younger and older adolescents in the degree to which they possess simple consumer-learning skills (Hypothesis 26). Third, it was expected that consumer-learning skills would be well integrated among older adolescents but not among younger adolescents (Hypothesis 27).

Table 28 shows age differences on complex consumer skills for younger and older adolescents. Older adolescents scored significantly higher than younger adolescents on five of the seven complex skills. Taken as a whole, these differences are statistically significant ($T^2 = 3.62$, $p < .001$) and support Hypothesis 25.

Although it was hypothesized that there would be no significant differences among younger and older adolescents in the degree to which they possess simple consumer skills, the data in Table 29 show that the two groups scored signifi-

Table 28: Age Differences on Complex Cognitive Consumer Skills Among Younger and Older Adolescents

Cognitive Consumer Skills	Younger Adolescents (N = 441)	Older Adolescents (N = 365)
Cognitive differentiation*	5.84	6.53
Puffery filtering*	28.03	28.39
Consumer finance management*	15.41	16.07
Information seeking*	11.17	12.07
Materialism	17.27	17.22
Social motivations	5.99	6.21
Economic motivations*	15.56	16.46

*Mean values for younger and older adolescents are significantly different using a one-tailed t-test with t .025 $>$ 1.96. For the specific level of significance see Table 9.
Note: Table entries are mean values for dependent variables in each group. The values are extracted from Table 9 for the reader's convenience. Hotteling's T^2 = 3.62, significant at .001 level.

cantly different on four of the six skills. Specifically, younger adolescents had more favorable attitudes toward three marketing stimuli (attitudes toward advertising, brands, and prices) and a lesser amount of consumer affairs knowledge than older adolescents. Overall, these differences were statistically significant (T^2 = 20.98, p < .001) and do not offer adequate support for Hypothesis 26. Thus even simple cognitive consumer skills appear to undergo formation and change during adolescence.

Table 29: Age Differences on Simple Cognitive Consumer Skills Among Younger and Older Adolescents

Cognitive Consumer Skills	Younger Adolescents (N = 441)	Older Adolescents (N = 365)
Attitudes toward advertising*	28.13	26.50
Attitudes toward brands*	14.58	13.95
Attitudes toward stores	10.54	10.82
Attitudes toward prices*	10.91	10.25
Attitudes toward salespeople	16.88	16.77
Consumer affairs knowledge*	5.37	6.54

*Mean values for younger and older adolescents are significantly different using a one-tailed t-test with t .025 $>$ 1.96. For the specific level of significance see Table 9.
Note: Table entries are mean values for dependent variables in each group. The values are extraced from Table 9 for the reader's convenience. Hotteling's T^2 = 20.98, significant at .001 level.

Table 30 shows product-moment correlations among consumer skill measures. The average correlation coefficient among younger adolescents was .09 (p < .07). The average correlation coefficient among older adolescents was .12 (p < .03). These results indicate that the intercorrelations among the cognitive consumer skill measures are well integrated only among older adolescents and support Hypothesis 27. The average correlations for older adolescents were significantly greater than the average correlations for younger adolescents (p < .02), suggesting that adolescents are continuously integrating these consumer skills as they grow older.

Relative Influence of Independent Variables

Because so much controversy appears to center around the relative influence of socialization agents on the learning of various consumer skills, the next consideration in this study was to provide data useful in answering such empirical questions. Furthermore, the investigation of the relative influence of the explanatory variables seemed necessary for providing data useful in (1) answering questions concerning the processes by which young people develop the ability to evaluate commercial stimuli and (2) accumulating research findings that could be used in formulating theory in the area.

The relative influence of the explanatory variables was assessed by means of multiple regression analysis. The adolescent's newspaper readership was used as a more general media-use variable to index the person's interaction with this print medium to make the analysis comparative to those of previous studies.[2] The newspaper readership variable was constructed by summing "very often to never" responses (measured on a 5-point scale) to the following items read in the newspaper: comics, sports, news about the government and politics, news about the economy, and advertisements. The coefficient alpha for this scale was .66.

A main limitation in using the multiple regression technique to assess the relative influence of the explanatory variables lies in the possible presence of intercorrelations among them, which can cause arbitrary allocation of the variance to the independent variables in a given equation. Table 31 shows that the correlations among the ten independent variables were rather low.[3] Thus the resulting regression coefficients in this analysis can be viewed as fairly accurate estimates of the

Table 30: Correlations Among Dependent Variables for Younger and Older Adolescents

	1	2	3	4	5	6	7	8	9	10	11	12	13
1. Advertising	—	.29	.19	.11	.26	-.03	.15	.09	-.06	.04	.17	.08	-.04
2. Brands	.07	—	.42	-.21	.11	-.19	-.12	-.08	-.11	.01	.25	.20	-.12
3. Stores	.05	.32	—	-.26	.15	-.15	-.09	-.11	-.01	-.02	.32	.16	-.16
4. Prices	.06	-.21	-.17	—	.13	.10	.13	.04	.10	.07	-.12	-.01	.10
5. Salespeople	.23	-.06	.07	.14	—	.05	.15	-.00	.02	.05	.01	-.06	.06
6. Consumer affairs	.01	-.07	-.01	.04	-.01	—	.05	.08	.07	.17	-.04	-.05	.25
7. Puffery filtering	-.06	-.13	-.08	.12	-.06	.03	—	.13	.18	.12	-.09	-.09	.21
8. Cognitive differentiation	.04	.01	.02	.02	.04	.24	.14	—	.13	.13	-.04	.22	-.00
9. Consumer finance	-.01	-.05	.02	.00	.06	.10	.07	.07	—	.16	.00	-.04	.25
10. Information seeking	.03	-.06	-.08	.11	.13	.12	.12	.06	.03	—	.12	.28	.37
11. Materialism	.12	.23	.26	-.23	.04	.13	-.13	.04	.02	.08	—	.22	-.00
12. Social motivations	.03	.06	.12	-.00	-.07	.02	-.07	-.03	-.03	.13	.07	—	.24
13. Economic motivations	-.02	-.11	-.08	.13	.01	.12	.17	.11	.07	.39	-.09	.24	—

Note: Table entries are product-moment correlations. Entries in the lower-left triangle of the matrix are correlations for the younger adolescents. Entries in the upper-right triangle are correlations for the older adolescents.

Values in the correlation matrix for the younger adolescents were compared to those values for the older adolescents by transforming them into Z scores and averaging. The average correlation coefficient among the dependent variables for older adolescents was significantly greater than the average correlation coefficient for the younger adolescents ($p < .021$).

Table 31: Correlation Matrix for Independent Variables

	1	2	3	4	5	6	7	8	9	10
1. Family communication	1.00									
2. Television viewing	.22	1.00								
3. Social utility reasons for watching TV shows	.18	.28	1.00							
4. Social utility reasons for watching TV ads	.12	.29	.54	1.00						
5. Newspaper reading	.11	.17	.02	-.01	1.00					
6. Peer communication	.33	.06	.17	.13	.14	1.00				
7. Courses	.11	.02	.01	.00	.11	.06	1.00			
8. Age	-.11	.08	-.16	-.21	.21	.13	.12	1.00		
9. Social class	.01	-.30	-.03	-.11	.08	.10	-.02	.09	1.00	
10. Sex	.07	-.04	.10	.09	-.12	.13	.28	-.05	.03	1.00

true effects of the respective variables on the consumer skills. Table 32 shows relationships between independent variables and each of the fourteen dependent consumer skill variables.

Attitudes Toward Advertising

The strongest predictor of this consumer skill was the adolescent's social utility reasons for watching television advertisements (b = .261, p < .001). Thus, to the extent to which advertisements offer gratifications of the child's social needs (e.g., provide a basis for interpersonal communications), the child tends to develop favorable attitudes toward advertising. Another strong predictor of adolescent attitudes toward advertising was peer communication about consumption (b = .116, p < .001). This relationship suggests that advertising may set the agenda for interpersonal communication with peers about consumption matters. Alternatively, the development of favorable advertising attitudes may be a consequence of more complex processes resulting from interpersonal processes.

Age was also an important predictor of advertising attitudes (b = −.104, p < .005). This negative relationship between the two variables suggests that adolescents may become more skeptical of advertising claims and develop a greater cognitive defense toward them as they grow older. Finally, consumer-related courses taken at school were fairly good predictors of advertising attitudes (b = .082, p < .018), suggesting that such courses may contain information concerning the positive aspects of advertising.

Attitudes Toward Brands

The strongest predictor of this consumer skill was the adolescent's social utility reasons for watching television advertisements (b = .241, p < .001). Adolescents who watch television commercials to gather information for social utility reasons are likely to develop and/or possess more favorable attitudes toward brands of products. The amount of television viewing is the second most significant predictor of brand attitudes (b = .131, p < .001), suggesting that mere exposure to the product brands advertised on television may be sufficient to create favorable attitudes toward them.

Table 32: Relationships Between Explanatory Variables and Dependent Consumer Skill Measures

	(1) Advertising	(2) Brands	(3) Stores	(4) Prices	(5) Salespeople	(6) Consumer Affairs	(7) Puffery Filtering	(8) Differentiation	(9) Information Seeking	(10) Finance Management	(11) Materialism	(12) Social Motives	(13) Economic Motives	(14) Consumer Activism
Independent Variables														*Dependent Variables*
TV viewing	.068	.131*	.016	-.102*	-.002	-.065	-.054	.113*	.015	-.039	.069	.099*	-.108*	-.011
Family communication	.002	-.052	.048	-.052	.038	-.060	-.071	-.027	-.026	.017	-.012	-.033	.059	.214*
Peer communication	.116*	.058	.040	.019	.052	.108*	.079*	.045	.099*	-.008	.121*	.138*	.027	.001
Courses	.083*	-.047	-.068	.047	.055	.015	-.028	.013	-.008	.033	-.009	.011	.046	-.041
Newspaper readership	.032	-.075	-.114*	.080*	.031	.236*	.092*	.169*	.091*	.080*	-.040	-.039	.166*	.306*
Social utility reasons for watching TV shows	-.000	-.091*	.071	.037	-.011	.088*	.097*	-.025	.114*	.022	.082*	.048	.122*	.034
Social utility reasons for watching TV ads	.261*	.241*	.072	-.050	.032	-.011	-.131*	.007	.036	-.022	.156*	.143*	-.078*	-.040
Age	-.104*	-.005	.107*	-.158*	-.003	.311*	.006	.140*	.074	.086*	.021	.020	.046	.110*
Social class	-.049	-.052	-.030	.052	.051	-.004	.082*	.068	.068	.112*	.033	.009	.085*	.001
Sex	.034	.016	-.121*	-.012	-.060	-.088*	.047	.161*	.062	.043	-.204*	-.133*	.041	.087*
Multiple R	.384	.296	.230	.173	.117	.486	.217	.314	.247	.201	.325	.281	.279	.420

Note: Table entries are standardized regression coefficients (beta-weights) between the independent variables and the fourteen dependent variables. Asterisk (*) denotes that the variable in the equation accounts for a significant amount of variance in the dependent variable (p = .05).

The least statistically significant predictors of brand attitudes were social utility reasons for watching television
programs (b = −.091, p < .027) and newspaper readership (b
= −.075, p < .040). Although these relationships appear
difficult to interpret in the absence of any concrete theory,
both explanatory variables have in common the information-
seeking aspect of the person's communication behavior. This
suggests that young people who seek more information from
the mass media may be more aware of alternatives and
evaluative purchasing criteria available to them and may
attach lesser significance to the product's brand name as a
criterion in purchasing decisions.

Attitudes Toward Stores

Sex was the strongest predictor of attitudes toward stores
(b = −.121, p < .001), suggesting that males tend to have
stronger favorable attitudes to such commercial stimuli than
females. Of equally significant importance and magnitude
was newspaper readership (b = −.114, p < .002), suggesting
that the newspaper media may be a dispenser of store-related
information, which makes young people aware of alternative
retail outlets. The last significant predictor of store attitudes
was age (b = .107, p < .006), suggesting that affective orientations toward stores may develop as a function of the
adolescent's cognitive development or experiences with
shopping and retail facilities.

Attitudes Toward Prices

Age was also an important predictor of attitudes toward
prices (b = −.158, p < .001). Perhaps the person's experience
with shopping increases his understanding of pricing tech-
niques in the marketplace, which in turn decreases his
confidence in price as an indicator of product quality or
performance. It is also possible that children may become
aware of other product attributes of equal or greater
importance in decision making, which also may lead to lower
evaluations of price as a significant attribute in decision
making.
    Heavy viewers of television are less likely to hold favorable
attitudes toward prices (b = −.102, p < .011), whereas

frequency of newspaper readership is positively related to favorability of attitudes toward prices (b = .080, p < .033).

Attitudes Toward Salespeople

No significant predictors of this consumer skill were revealed. This finding suggests that the formation of attitudes toward salespeople may be occurring in a positive direction for some adolescents and in a negative direction for others.

Consumer Affairs Knowledge

Age was the strongest predictor of the adolescent's consumer affairs knowledge (b = .311, p < .001), suggesting that the acquisition of this skill may be the result of the cognitive developmental process. Newspaper readership also correlates strongly with consumer affairs knowledge (b = .236, p < .001). Thus it appears that the newspaper may be a significant learning source for consumption-related matters for adolescents. Adolescents also appear to acquire such knowledge from their peers (b = .108, p < .001) and from television by watching shows for social utility reasons (b = .088, p < .008). Finally, male adolescents appear to possess a significantly greater amount of consumer affairs knowledge than do female adolescents (b = −.088, p < .008).

Puffery Filtering

Adolescents who watch television commercials for social utility reasons are less likely to be able to filter puffery in advertising (b = −.131, p < .002) than those who do not watch for such reasons. Nevertheless, those who watch television programs for social utility reasons appear to possess this skill to a significantly greater extent than those who do not (b = .097, p < .022). This skill is also positively related to newspaper readership (b = .092, p < .014), social class (b = .082, p < .021), and communication with peers (b = .079, p < .039). (The results on filtering puffery should be interpreted with great caution. Not only was the reliability coefficient rather low [.25], but also it is not clear whether the measure itself actually measures puffery. Those respondents scoring high on "puffery" statements tended to score low on "factual" statements, suggesting that this scale may in effect be a more general measure of believability of advertising claims.)

Cognitive Differentiation

Two media-use variables were strong predictors of this consumer skill: newspaper readership (b = .169, p < .001) and television viewing (b = .113, p < .003). Given the nature of the measure for this skill, these predictors could best be viewed as control rather than explanatory variables, i.e., exposure to mass media is a necessary condition for learning this skill. Sex and age could best be considered the true explanatory variables. Females seem to have a greater ability to remember commercial stimuli (b = .161, p < .001) than do males. This ability also may be acquired as a result of maturation (b = .140, p < .001).

Information Seeking

Three communication variables accounted for a significant amount of variance in this dependent consumer skill. The strongest predictor was the adolescent's social utility reasons for watching television shows (b = .114, p < .006), followed by communication with peers about consumption matters (b = .099, p < .009) and newspaper readership (b = .091, p < .015). Taken together, these findings show that adolescents who actively seek information from the media and from peers are also likely to seek information before they make a decision. All three antecedent variables approached significance. Upper class adolescents are more likely to seek a greater amount of information than are lower class adolescents (b = .068, p < .052). Similarly, older adolescents tend to seek more information prior to decision making than do younger adolescents (b = .074, p < .058). Finally, female adolescents appear to seek more information for decision making than do male adolescents (b = .067, p < .092).

Consumer Finance Management

The amount of the child's interaction with the various socialization agents seems to have little to do with the learning of this skill. Only newspaper readership is rather weakly related to the adolescent's ability to manage consumer finances (b = .080, p < .033). Stronger predictors of this skill are social class (b = .112, p < .002) and age (b = .086, p < .029), suggesting that adolescents from upper classes and of older age are more likely to possess this ability than their lower class and younger counterparts.

Materialism

Male adolescents had significantly more favorable attitudes toward materialism than did female adolescents (b = −.204, p < .001). Aside from sex, only the media (television in particular) and peers appeared to influence the development of materialistic values. However, the influence of the mass media may be in the form of social utility reasons for watching television advertisements (b = .156, p < .001) and shows (b = .082, p < .042) rather than being a simple stimulus-response phenomenon, because the frequency of the child's exposure to television is weakly related to materialism (b = .069, p < .072). Peers are apparently a strong influence on other adolescents in learning materialistic attitudes (b = .121, p < .001).

Social Motivations for Consumption

The media and peers also were found to be important socialization agents in teaching the adolescent social motives for consumption. The strength of social motivations for consumption was strongly related to motivations for watching television advertisements (b = .143, p < .001) and exposure to television (b = .099, p < .011); it was not related significantly to motivations for watching television shows for social utility reasons. These findings suggest that the learning of such orientations may be affected by television advertising, whereas the influence of television commercials seems to be not only hypodermic but also a second-order consequence that is conditioned by interpersonal social processes. This reasoning is also supported by the positive significant relationship found between this consumer skill and the frequency of the adolescent's communication with his peers about consumption matters (b = .138, p < .001). Finally, sex is an equally strong predictor (b = −.133, p < .001), suggesting that male adolescents develop social motives for consumption to a significantly greater extent (or faster) than female adolescents.

Economic Motivations for Consumption

The mass media seems to be an important information source from which young people acquire economic motivations for consumption. Newspaper readership was the strongest predictor (b = .166, p < .001), closely followed by social utility motivations for watching television programs (b = .122, p < .003). The amount of exposure to television (hence the number of advertisements) and social utility reasons for watching television commercials were negatively related to such motives (b = −.108, p < .006 and b = −.078, p < .002, respectively). These findings suggest that television advertising may be a constraint to the adolescent's development of "rational" motivations for consumption. Social class is also a strong predictor (b = .085, p < .015), suggesting that upper class adolescents are more likely to possess such motivations than their lower class counterparts.

Consumer Activism

The amount of newspaper reading was the strongest predictor of the adolescent's "socially desirable" consumer behaviors (b = .306, p < .001). Most families also appear to emphasize such behaviors in their conversations with children about consumption matters (b = .214, p < .001). Age, on the other hand, indexing the adolescent's ability to perform such desirable acts (e.g., shopping around before buying something that costs a lot of money), may be viewed as a facilitating or control variable (b = .110, p < .003). The analysis also showed that female adolescents engaged in such activities to a significantly greater extent than did their male counterparts (b = .087, p < .012).

---

1. For the rationale of including significant antecedent variables in the analysis as "control" variables, see Chapter 2, "Explanatory Variables," p. 15.

2. Roy L. Moore and Lowndes F. Stephens, "Some Communication and Demographic Determinants of Adolescent Consumer Learning," *Journal of Consumer Research*, September 1975, pp. 80-92; and Scott Ward and Daniel B. Wackman, "Family and Media Influences on Adolescent Consumer Learning," *American Behavioral Scientist*, January-February 1971, pp. 415-427.

3. Further evidence of relatively low intercorrelations among the predictor variables can be found by examining the successive eigenvalues. The sum of the reciprocals of the ten eigenvalues is 12.52, a value which is nearly what it would be for an orthogonal system. See Arthur E. Hoerl and Robert W. Kennard, "Ridge Regression: Biased Estimation for Nonorthogonal Problems," *Technometrics*, February 1970, pp. 69-82.

Chapter **5**

A Causal Model of
Consumer Socialization

The final consideration in this research was the development and empirical test of a causal model of consumer socialization. The discussion of main variables in Chapter 2 as well as previous theoretical and empirical work in the area[1] suggested a general conceptual framework of consumer socialization, which is shown in Figure 1. Conceptually, consumer skills may be viewed as dependent variables; social structural factors and maturation may be considered independent variables. Socialization processes, which incorporate two main types of variables (elements)—the socialization agent and the learning process(es) actually operating—may be viewed as intervening variables.

In developing the causal model in this research, three criterion variables are investigated: *economic motivations for consumption, social motivations for consumption,* and *materialistic values.* These variables were selected not only because of their relevance to contemporary consumer socialization issues but also because such motivations and values are believed to be central skills defining the person's orientation toward consumption in general[2] and consumer role in particular.[3] Because of the cross-sectional nature of this study, only the *social interaction* learning process is investigated. This process is conceptualized in line with previous cross-sectional studies[4] in terms of the learner's frequency of

Figure 1: A Conceptual Model of Consumer Socialization

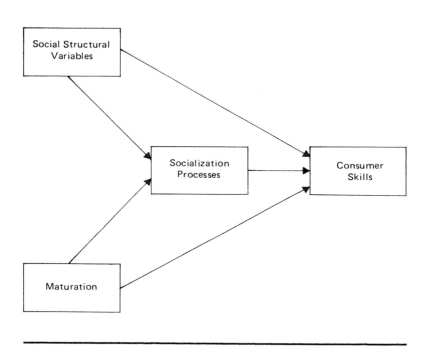

interaction with three agents believed to be important in consumer socialization research: *television, parents,* and *peers.*[5] The social structural constraints investigated are *social class, sex,* and *birth order.* Previous theory and research suggest these variables may be important antecedents in consumer socialization.[6]

Research findings in several disciplinary areas suggest the following causal model. First, with respect to the influence of the antecedent variables, as children grow older, they spend less time with television,[7] and they interact more frequently with their peers[8] and less frequently with their parents about consumption matters.[9] It is also hypothesized that consumer learning is, at least partly, a matter of cognitive development.[10] Furthermore, as the family's socioeconomic status increases, young people are expected to interact more frequently with their parents about consumption matters.[11] This type of interaction is expected to be more frequent among the first born than the later born children; the latter group is expected to interact more frequently with their peers.[12] Female adolescents are expected to talk about consumption matters more frequently than male adolescents.[13] They also are expected to be more susceptible to social influence than their male counterparts.[14]

As a socialization agent, television is expected to *directly* affect the adolescent's acquisition of "expressive" aspects of consumption (materialism and social motivations)[15] and *indirectly* the "goal-directed" elements of consumption (economic or rational motivations) by setting up the agenda for positive parent-child interactions at home.[16] Family, on the other hand, is expected to contribute to the child's learning of only the goal-directed elements of the consumer role[17] and to provide a basis for interpersonal communication with the individual's peers, although peer and parent-child communication about consumption may be reciprocal.[18] Peers as socializing agents are expected to influence the child's acquisition of expressive elements of the consumer role.[19]

The previous discussion suggests the conceptual diagram in Figure 2 as a model of the process of consumer socialization. Figure 2 in turn suggests that the following structural equations need to be solved in order to assess the sources of the various consumption influences:

X_1, X_2, X_3, X_4 exogenous.

$$X_5 = \beta_{51} X_1 + \mu_5 \tag{1}$$

$$X_6 = \beta_{61} X_1 + \beta_{62} X_2 + \beta_{63} X_3 + \beta_{65} X_5 + \beta_{67} X_7 + \mu_6 \tag{2}$$

$$X_7 = \beta_{71} X_1 + \beta_{73} X_3 + \beta_{74} X_4 + \beta_{75} X_5 + \beta_{76} X_6 + \mu_7 \tag{3}$$

$$X_8 = \beta_{81} X_1 + \beta_{84} X_4 + \beta_{85} X_5 + \beta_{87} X_7 + \mu_8 \tag{4}$$

$$X_9 = \beta_{91} X_1 + \beta_{94} X_4 + \beta_{95} X_5 + \beta_{97} X_7 + \mu_9 \tag{5}$$

$$X_{10} = \beta_{101} X_1 + \beta_{106} X_6 + \mu_{10} \tag{6}$$

Three of the exogenous variables (age, birth order, and sex) were treated as dummy variables; age and birth order were dichotomized so as to be consistent with previous research,[20]

Figure 2: Conceptual Model of Consumer Socialization Process

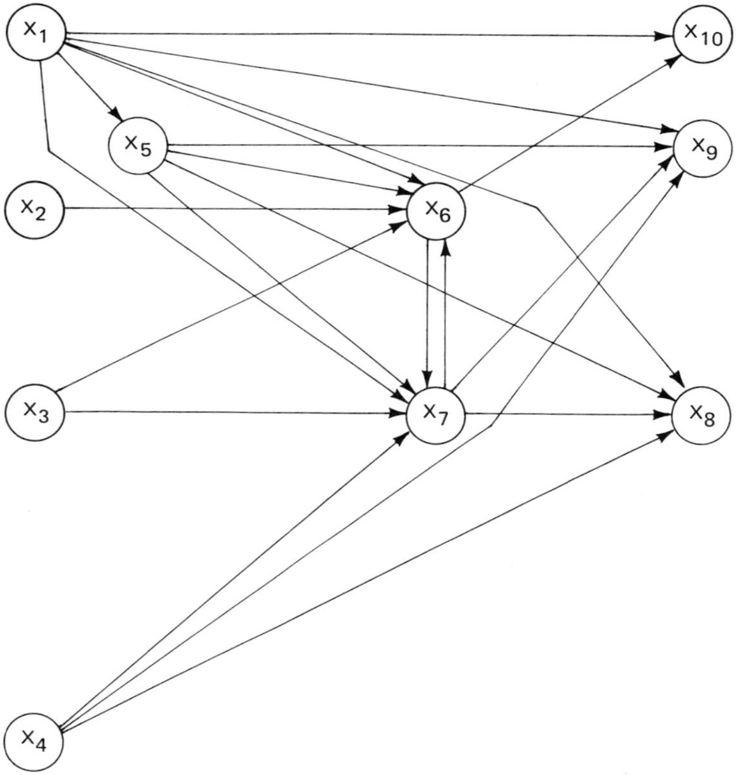

X_1 = Age
X_2 = Socioeconomic Status
X_3 = Birth Order
X_4 = Sex
X_5 = Amount of Television Viewing
X_6 = Family Communication About Consumption
X_7 = Peer Communication About Consumption
X_8 = Materialism
X_9 = Social Motivations for Consumption
X_{10} = Economic Motivations for Consumption

and sex is naturally dichotomous. More specifically, these three variables were coded as follows:

Age
X_1 = 1 if respondent was over 15 and thus an older adolescent.
0 if respondent was under 15 and thus a younger adolescent.

Birth Order
X_3 = 1 if respondent had no older brothers or sisters.
0 if respondent had an older brother or sister.

Sex
X_4 = 1 if respondent was female.
0 if respondent was male.

The path analytic diagram of Figure 2 suggests that the system of equations is nonrecursive. Family communication about consumption (X_6) affects, and is simultaneously affected by, peer communication about consumption (X_7). Consequently, ordinary least squares could not be used to estimate the coefficients because the technique produces biased, inconsistent estimates,[21] and two-stage least squares regression is the recommended approach.

In two-stage least squares regression, one regresses the endogenous variables in the troublesome equations on *all* of the exogenous variables. The *estimated* value of the endogenous variables is then inserted in the appropriate equation and ordinary least squares regression is used to secure coefficient estimates.

In our case, the troublesome equations are those for X_6 and X_7. The coefficients in these equations were therefore estimated by:

1. Regressing X_6 on X_1, X_2, X_3, X_4 and X_7 on X_1, X_2, X_3, X_4.

2. Estimating the coefficients in the regression equations:

$$X_6 = \beta_{61}X_1 + \beta_{62}X_2 + \beta_{63}X_3 + \beta_{65}X_5 + \beta_{67}\hat{X}_7 + \mu_6$$

$$X_7 = \beta_{71}X_1 + \beta_{73}X_3 + \beta_{74}X_4 + \beta_{75}X_5 + \beta_{76}\hat{X}_6 + \mu_7$$

where $\hat{X}_6$ and $\hat{X}_7$ were now the estimated values based on the first stage regression.

It was not necessary to solve for the coefficients in the X_8, X_9, and X_{10} equations this way, because the model is block recursive.[22] Equations 4-6 were thus solved by the ordinary least squares method, as was equation 1.

The results of the estimating procedure are displayed in Table 33. The reported coefficients are raw score coefficients and not standardized regression coefficients in keeping with Duncan's suggestion that "it would probably be salutary if research workers relinquished the habit of expressing variables in standard form. The main reason for this recommendation is that standardization *tends to obscure the distinction between the structural coefficients of the model and the several variances and covariances that describe the joint distribution of the variables in a certain population.*"[23] Although the results are generally consistent with the structured model, they are not entirely so. The amount of television viewing among adolescents (X_5) does decline with age as hypothesized. Furthermore, family communication about consumption matters (X_6) declines with age, increases with the amount of television viewing, and increases with the amount of peer communication about consumption, all as posited. However, the impact of socioeconomic status on family communications is negative, although the coefficient is not statistically significant. It was hypothesized to be positive. The impact of birth order on family communication about consumption is estimated to be positive as hypothesized, but the relationship is not significant.

With respect to peer communication about consumption (X_7), there is one deviation from the model. The impact of sex is not significant, indicating that females do not discuss consumption matters more than males. Consumption-related peer communication does increase, though, with age, with the amount of television viewing, and with the amount of family communication about consumption, and decreases among other than first-born children, all as hypothesized.

The sources of materialism (X_8) were generally consistent with what was proposed in the model; materialistic values did increase with the amount of television viewing and with the extent of peer communication. However, females display

Table 33: Hypothesized (H) and Estimated (E) Relationships Between Variables

Predictor Variable	X_5		X_6		X_7		X_8		X_9		X_{10}	
	H	E	H	E	H	E	H	E	H	E	H	E
X_1	−	−7.57*	−	−.401††	+	1.702*	+	−.047	+	.029	+	4.11*
X_2			+	−.005								
X_3			+	.604	−	−.972††						
X_4					+	−1.598	+	−1.646*	+	−1.117*		
X_5			+	.296*	+	.118*	−	.101†	+	.125*		
X_6					+	3.485†					+	.087†
X_7			+	.832††			+	.150*	+	.154*		
R^2		.089*		.050*		.054*		.061*		.047*		.020*

*Significant at the .001 level.
†Significant at the .01 level.
††Significant at the .05 level.

⌐_⌐ Inconsistent with hypothesized model.

Figure 3: Revised Model of Consumer Socialization Process Based on the Path Analytic Investigation

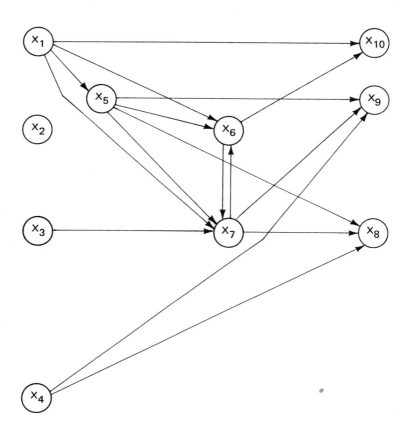

X_1 = Age
X_2 = Socioeconomic Status
X_3 = Birth Order
X_4 = Sex
X_5 = Amount of Television Viewing
X_6 = Family Communication About Consumption
X_7 = Peer Communication About Consumption
X_8 = Materialism
X_9 = Social Motivations for Consumption
X_{10} = Economic Motivations for Consumption

lower materialistic orientations than do males, a finding that is opposite to what was hypothesized. The estimated impact of age was opposite in sign to that proposed, but the coefficient was not significant.

Age also did not affect a respondent's social motivations for consumption (X_9), as posited. The coefficient was in the right direction but was not significant. Females displayed significantly weaker social consumption motives than males, which is opposite to what was hypothesized. The amount of television viewing and the amount of peer communication positively impacted a respondent's social motivations for consumption.

Economic motivations for consumption (X_{10}) were positively related to age and the amount of family communication about consumption matters, as posited. The results in Table 33 lead to the reformulation of the model as shown in Figure 3.

---

1. George P. Moschis and Roy L. Moore, "An Analysis of the Acquisition of Some Consumer Competencies Among Adolescents," *Journal of Consumer Affairs*, forthcoming; and George P. Moschis and Gilbert A. Churchill, Jr., "Consumer Socialization: A Theoretical and Empirical Analysis," *Journal of Marketing Research*, forthcoming.

2. Raymond A. Bauer, "The Obstinate Audience: The Influence Process from the Point of View of Social Communication," *American Psychologist*, May 1964, pp. 319-328.

3. David Riesman and Howard Roseborough, "Careers and Consumer Behavior," in Lincoln Clark, ed., *Consumer Behavior*, Vol. II, *The Life Cycle and Consumer Behavior* (New York: New York University Press, 1955).

4. Scott Ward and Daniel B. Wackman, "Family and Media Influences on Adolescent Consumer Learning," *American Behavioral Scientist*, January-February 1971, pp. 415-427; Roy L. Moore and Lowndes F. Stephens, "Some Communication and Demographic Determinants of Adolescent Consumer Learning," *Journal of Consumer Research*, September 1975, pp. 80-92; and Moschis and Moore, "An Analysis of the Acquisition of Some Consumer Competencies Among Adolescents."

5. Scott Ward, "Consumer Socialization," *Journal of Consumer Research*, September 1974, pp. 1-14.

6. Ibid.

7. Wilbur Schramm, Jack Lyle, and Edwin B. Parker, *Television in the Lives of our Children* (Stanford, California: Stanford University Press, 1961); Moore and Stephens, "Some Communication and Demographic Determinants of Adolescent Consumer Learning"; R. Moore and G. Moschis, "Teenagers' Reactions to Advertising," *Journal of Advertising*, forthcoming; and Ward and Wackman, "Family and Media Influences on Adolescent Consumer Learning."

8. Roy L. Moore, George P. Moschis, and Lowndes F. Stephens, "An Exploratory Study of Consumer Role Perceptions in Adolescent Consumer Socialization," Paper presented to the International Communication Association, Chicago, April 1975; and Moore and Moschis, "Teenagers' Reactions to Advertising."

9. Ward and Wackman, "Family and Media Influences on Adolescent Consumer Learning."

10. Lawrence Kohlberg, "The Cognitive Developmental Approach to Socialization," in D.A. Goslin, ed., *Handbook of Socialization Theory and Research* (Chicago: Rand McNally and Co., 1969); and Moore and Stephens, "Some Communication and Demographic Determinants of Adolescent Consumer Learning."

11. Scott Ward, Daniel Wackman, and Ellen Wartella, *How Children Learn to Buy* (Beverly Hills, California: Sage Publications, 1977), pp. 134-135.

12. Jerome Kagan, "The Child in the Family," in *Daedalus*, American Academy of Arts and Sciences, Spring 1977, pp. 33-56.

13. Philip R. Cateora, *An Analysis of the Teenage Market* (Austin, Texas: Bureau of Business Research, University of Texas, 1963); Janice Hamilton and Jessie Warden, "Student's Role in a High School Community and His Clothing Behavior," *Journal of Home Economics*, December 1966, pp. 781-791; C.A. Millson, "Conformity to Peers Versus Adults in Early Adolescence," Doctoral Dissertation (New York: Cornell University, 1966); and Josephine R. Sanders, A. Coskum Salmi, and Enid F. Tozier, "Congruence and Conflict in Buying Decisions of Mothers and Daughters," *Journal of Retailing*, Fall 1973, pp. 3-18.

14. Kenneth C. Cannon, Ruth Staples, and Irene Carlson, "Personal Appearance as a Factor in Personal Acceptance," *Journal of Home Economics*, November 1952, pp. 710-713; and George P. Moschis, Roy L. Moore, and Lowndes F. Stephens, "Purchasing Patterns of Adolescent Consumers," *Journal of Retailing*, Spring 1977, pp. 17-26.

15. Albert Bandura, "Modeling Influences on Children," Testimony to the Federal Trade Commission, November 1971.

16. T. Parsons, R.F. Bales, and E.A. Shils, *Working Papers in the Theory of Action* (Glencoe, Illinois: Free Press, 1953); and David Riesman and Howard Roseborough, "Careers and Consumer Behavior."

17. Riesman and Roseborough, "Careers and Consumer Behavior"; and Ward, Wackman, and Wartella, *How Children Learn to Buy*.

18. Moore, Moschis, and Stephens, "An Exploratory Study of Consumer Role Perceptions in Adolescent Consumer Socialization"; and Moore and Moschis, "Teenagers' Reactions to Advertising."

19. Parsons, Bales, and Shils, *Working Papers in the Theory of Action*; and Riesman and Roseborough, "Careers and Consumer Behavior."

20. Kohlberg, "The Cognitive Developmental Approach to Socialization"; Ward and Wackman, "Family and Media Influences on Adolescent Consumer Learning"; Moore and Stephens, "Some Communication and Demographic Determinants of Adolescent Consumer Learning"; and Kagan, "The Child in the Family."

21. Otis D. Duncan, *Introduction to Structural Equation Models* (New York: Academic Press, 1975); and Eric A. Hannshek and John E. Jackson, *Statistical Methods for Social Scientists* (New York: Academic Press, 1977).

22. Duncan, *Introduction to Structural Equation Models*, p. 85 (emphasis added).

23. Ibid., p. 51.

Chapter 6

Discussion of Research Findings

This research in adolescent consumer socialization was guided by two models of socialization: the social learning model and the cognitive developmental model. The social learning model focuses on sources of influence—commonly known as "socialization agents"—transmitting attitudes, motives, and values to the learner. Learning is assumed to be taking place during the person's interaction with socialization agents in various social settings. The cognitive developmental model, on the other hand, views learning as a cognitive psychological process of adjustment to one's environment. Learning is assumed to occur as a function of the person's maturation or cognitive development indexed by his age. In other words, at a certain age a person will automatically have learned a group of consumer behaviors and cognitions.

Consumer Socialization as a Social Process

Using the social learning approach to adolescent consumer socialization, this investigator examined the influence of family, television, peers, and school on the development of selected consumer skills.

Family Influences

Family appears to be important in teaching adolescents "rational" aspects of consumption. The data showed a significant positive relationship between the amount of intrafamily communication about consumption and the extent to which adolescents held economic motivations for consumption. The findings appear to be consistent with speculations of some sociologists with respect to the kinds of consumer behaviors young people learn from their parents.[1]

In addition, this research found a strong positive relationship between intrafamily communication about consumption and the adolescent's frequency of performing socially desirable consumer acts. Although previous researchers have reported that parents purposely teach their children (5 to 12 year olds) very little about consumption but rather expect them to learn some skills through observation,[2] the findings of this research suggest that parents may purposely attempt to teach consumer skills to their teen-aged youngsters. Thus different consumer skills may be learned at different ages from parents and through different learning processes.

Mass Media Influences

The amount of *television viewing*, and consequently the number of television advertisements to which adolescents were exposed, predicted the strength of favorability of attitudes toward advertising and brands in general. These findings suggest that overexposure to marketing stimuli may result in favorable affective orientations toward them and that the hypodermic model of communication effects may partly explain the acquisition of these simple skills. The amount of television viewing was also a good predictor of the respondent's social motivations for consumption and materialistic attitudes, suggesting that mere exposure to this medium also may result to a significant extent in the learning of complex skills.

Although the adolescent's frequency of interaction with television appears to be an important factor in learning some simple and complex skills, it is questionable whether exposure to the medium alone is sufficient. These data showed that learning from television occurred mainly as a function of the uses the adolescent makes of television, especially of commercial content, much of which was assumed and found to be social in nature. These findings are consistent with those of previous research studies.[3]

This research also supports Bandura's and others' contention that young people learn the "expressive" or "adaptive" elements of consumption from television.[4] However, the learning of these skills may not develop through imitation and observation alone, as Bandura argues. Rather, social processes (e.g., communications with peers) may condition adolescents' perceptions and interest in goods and services, which in turn cause them to pay more attention to television programs and commercials to learn about social uses of products. Thus the transactional model of communication effects seems to best describe the learning of consumer skills from television.[5]

Newspaper readership was a strong predictor of the adolescent's consumer affairs knowledge, cognitive differentiation of television advertising, economic motivations for consumption, consumer activism, puffery filtering, information seeking, and consumer finance management. Although it is tempting to assume that adolescents develop these consumer skills *because* they read the newspaper, it is possible that a reverse causality may be at work—i.e., newspaper readership may be a function of the consumer skills, knowledge, and attitudes already acquired. It also is possible that a *third variable* may be present here. For example, a family environment that allows and/or encourages newspaper readership might also foster the development of desirable consumer skills, making both the readership and the skills learning dependent on the third variable—the family environment.[6] A similar interpretation could be given to the findings regarding the positive relationship between the amount of *public affairs* media use and the adolescent's consumer affairs knowledge.

To summarize, different kinds of mass media, apparently used for different reasons, may lead to the learning of different consumer skills. Learning may only partially be a matter of a stimulus-response phenomenon occurring simply as a function of the amount of television viewing; and other variables may affect the adolescent's learning from the mass media.

Peer Influence

Peers appear to be an important socialization agent. Besides the expressive elements of consumption (i.e., social motivations) that adolescents may learn from their peers, interaction with peers also seems to lead to materialistic attitudes. These results suggest that the adolescents' communication with their peers about consumption matters may focus on the social importance of goods and services; and it may be a second-order consequence of learning from parents rather than from television. For example, the correlation between intrafamily communication about consumption and communication with peers was relatively high ($r = .33$); television viewing was weakly associated with peer communication about consumption ($r = .06$) (Table 31).

Adolescents might learn not only the expressive aspects of consumption from their peers but also many other skills. Interpersonal communication with peers seems to lead to the learning of many positive aspects of consumer behavior. It may contribute to the adolescent's knowledge about consumer affairs; it may increase his ability to cognitively filter puffery in advertising; and it may motivate him to seek a greater amount of information prior to decision making. In addition, communication with peers about consumption may contribute to the development of favorable attitudes toward advertising. These findings suggest that interpersonal interaction with peers about consumption matters may make the adolescent aware of goods and services in the marketplace and of the buying processes. This greater awareness of his consumer environment may in turn contribute to his *active* interaction about consumption matters with other socialization agents such as the mass media, which in turn may result in additional learning. For example, the correlations between social utility reasons for viewing television programs and commercials were significantly related to the frequency of the adolescent's interaction with his peers ($r = .13$, $p < .001$ and $r = .17$, $p < .001$, respectively) (Table 31).

The Influence of School

This study found little evidence that formal consumer education contributes much to the adolescent's learning of various consumer skills, a finding that is consistent with the results of a large number of studies of the effectiveness of consumer education.[7] At least three possible factors might account for this finding. First, the instructional material may not contain information useful in teaching the young people the effective aspects of the consumer role as defined in this research. Second, instructors may be using ineffective methods of teaching socially desirable consumer skills. Third, some other variable is associated with the student's propensity to take consumer-related courses; for example, students who make poor grades at school (are not as capable of learning) might perceive such courses to have a low degree of difficulty. Other researchers have pointed out the first two possibilities.[8]

Consumer Socialization as a Cognitive Developmental Process

On the basis of the cognitive developmental approach to socialization, this researcher investigated (a) the adolescents' levels of competence on various consumer skills and (b) the integration of these skills.

Contrary to the cognitive developmental model (especially Piaget's theory of intellectual development), which assumes that most socialization has taken place by the age of 15, this research found that consumer socialization continues throughout the late adolescent years. Both younger and older adolescents appear to develop and integrate simple and complex consumer skills continuously (Table 1), suggesting that the various consumer skills may be learned together. This continuous learning and integration of skills may be the result of the adolescents' frequency of interaction with the marketplace, either on their own (e.g., as a result of purchasing experience) or by accompanying others; or they may simply reflect the integration of cognitive skills in general, not just consumer skills.[9] It also is possible that the cognitive developmental approach to socialization may simply be referring to more primary development, whereas the cognitive skills studied in this research may be more secondary. Overall, the findings suggest that the cognitive approach to consumer socialization may be of relatively little value in future studies of adolescent consumer learning.

It should be noted, however, that age was a fairly strong predictor for several consumer skills. For example, age predicted the development of attitudes toward advertising, stores, and prices; it was the strongest predictor of the adolescent's consumer affairs knowledge; and it predicted fairly well the child's ability to cognitively differentiate advertising stimuli, manage consumer finances, and perform socially desirable consumer acts. It is not clear, however, whether these changes in the youth are the effects of cognitive development or of other variables, such as opportunity for consumption and ability to perform certain consumer acts.[10] Thus age as a surrogate index of cognitive development can be used in a predictive, but not in an explanatory, sense.

In summary, cognitive development may predict the acquisition of some consumer skills, such as cognitive defense toward commercials, but in itself it may not completely or accurately explain consumer socialization. Age may serve as an important condition for some kinds of consumer learning, but age alone does not seem to be sufficient.

Effects of Social Structural Variables

This study examined the effects of two social structural constraints, social class and sex. It was speculated that adolescents from higher socioeconomic families have more opportunities for consumption and, therefore, would be socialized faster and better to the consumption role. The data presented in this study appear to partly support this line of reasoning. Upper social class adolescents had a greater ability to filter puffery in advertising and to manage consumer finances, and they had greater economic motivations for consumption than did lower class adolescents. The data presented in this study unfortunately did not indicate whether better consumer learning occurs as a result of structural factors present in higher socioeconomic classes (e.g., greater opportunities for consumption) or because of different socialization practices that may be emphasized by families in these social groups.

Most differences between the sexes revealed in this study suggest that adolescent males learn the consumer role to a significantly greater extent than their female counterparts. Male adolescents were found to possess more favorable attitudes toward stores, they had a greater amount of consumer affairs knowledge, and they possessed stronger materialistic attitudes and social motivations for consumption than female adolescents. Females, on the other hand, appeared to perform more socially desirable consumer acts and they could differentiate advertising stimuli better than male adolescents. The latter findings appear to support the contention that females have a better memory than males.[11] It is also possible that females may possess the ability to make discriminations to a significantly greater extent than male adolescents, or that females are more attuned to advertising than are males.[12]

Finally, the data provided support for the causal model of consumer socialization presented. Some relationships between variables were in the opposite direction than what was hypothesized, but most of these were not statistically significant. Age, sex, and birth order appear to be significant antecedent variables of consumer socialization. The influence of sex appears to be direct, whereas the influence of age and birth order seems to be primarily indirect—i.e., by influencing socialization processes. The findings of the path analytic investigation further highlight the family's mediating function in the socialization process.[13] But the findings also suggest that it would be unreasonable to assume that outside-the-home influences, like television and peers, are filtered and interpreted by the young person in a family setting. Rather, such socialization agents also appear to affect the individual's consumer learning directly.

---

1. T. Parsons, R.F. Bales, and E.A. Shils, *Working Papers in the Theory of Action* (Glencoe, Illinois: The Free Press, 1953); and David Riesman and Howard Roseborough, "Careers and Consumer Behavior," in Lincoln Clark, ed., *Consumer Behavior Vol. II, The Life Cycle and Consumer Behavior* (New York: New York University Press, 1955).

2. Scott Ward and Daniel B. Wackman, "Effects of Television Advertising on Consumer Socialization," Working Paper (Cambridge, Massachusetts: Marketing Science Institute, 1973).

3. Scott Ward and Daniel B. Wackman, "Family and Media Influences on Adolescent Consumer Learning," *American Behavioral Scientist*, January-February 1971, pp. 415-427; and Roy L. Moore and Lowndes F. Stephens, "Some Communication and Demographic Determinants of Adolescent Consumer Learning," *Journal of Consumer Research*, September 1975, pp. 80-92.

4. Albert Bandura, "Modeling Influences on Children," Testimony to the Federal Trade Commission, November 1971; Parsons, Bales, and Shils, *Working Papers in the Theory of Action*; and Riesman and Roseborough, "Careers and Consumer Behavior."

5. Jack M. McLeod and Lee B. Becker, "Testing the Validity of Media Gratifications Through Political Effects Analysis," in J.G. Blumler and E. Katz, eds., *The Uses of Mass Communication* (Beverly Hills, California: Sage Publications, 1974).

6. See, for example, Steven H. Chaffee, Jack M. McLeod, and Charles K. Atkin, "Parental Influences on Adolescent Media Use," *American Behavioral Scientist*, January-February 1971, pp. 323-340.

7. Roy L. Moore, George P. Moschis, and Lowndes F. Stephens, "An Exploratory Study of Consumer Role Perceptions in Adolescent Consumer Socialization," paper presented to the International Communication Association Conference, Chicago, 1975; George P. Moschis and Roy L. Moore, "An Analysis of the Acquisition of Some Consumer Competencies Among Adolescents," *Journal of Consumer Affairs*, forthcoming; F.W. Langrehr and J.B. Mason, "The Development and Implementation of the Concept of Consumer Education," *Journal of Consumer Affairs*, Winter 1977, pp. 63-79; and Calvin H. Hawkins, "A Study of the Use of Consumer Education Concepts by High School Graduates," *Journal of Consumer Affairs*, Summer 1977, pp. 122-127.

8. H.R. Marshall and Lucille Magruder, "Relations Between Parent Money Education Practices and Children's Knowledge and Use of Money," *Child Development*, Vol. 31, 1960, pp. 253-284; S.L. Diamond, "Consumer Education: Perspectives on the State of the Art," unpublished paper (Cambridge, Massachusetts: Harvard University, Graduate School of Business Administration, 1974); and Scott Ward, "Consumer Socialization," *Journal of Consumer Research*, September 1974, pp. 1-14.

9. Moore and Stephens, "Some Communication and Demographic Determinants of Adolescent Consumer Learning," p. 86.

10. Orville G. Brim, "Socialization Through the Life Cycle," in O. Brim and S. Wheeler, eds., *Socialization After Childhood* (New York: John Wiley & Sons, Inc., 1966).

11. R.S. Alexander, "Some Aspects of Sex Differences in Relation to Marketing," *Journal of Marketing*, July 1947, pp. 158-172.

12. I.L. Janis and P.B. Field, "Sex Differences and Personality," in C. Hovland and I. Janis, eds., *Personality and Persuasibility* (New Haven, Connecticut: Yale University Press, 1955), pp. 55-68.

13. James F. Engel, Roger D. Blackwell, and David T. Kollat, *Consumer Behavior*, 2nd ed. (Hinsdale, Illinois: The Dryden Press, 1973).

Chapter 7

Summary, Implications, and Directions for Future Research

This chapter is divided into three parts. The first part summarizes the main sections of this study: rationale, purpose, research approach, and findings. The second part discusses implications of the study for marketers, public policy makers, consumer educators, and students of socialization and consumer behavior. The last part of the chapter suggests directions for future research.

Summary

Rationale for the Study

This study was concerned with the development of consumption-related skills, knowledge, and attitudes during adolescence. Interest in this area of research developed as a result of various contemporary issues relating to public and corporate strategy formulation. One issue that served as a rationale for this study was of main interest to public policy makers and was related to the effects of the mass media, parents, and peers on young people's consumer learning. Another rationale for this research was based on the industry's need for understanding consumer behavior among young people as a means of designing effective and efficient marketing communications directed at them. Issues relating to the effectiveness of current consumer education materials and practices in teaching young people effective consumer behaviors, which were of main interest to consumer educators, served as another justification for the research. The last rationale for this study was based on a purely theoretical issue of interest to students of socialization and consumer behavior regarding the process(es) by which young people acquire consumption-related skills, knowledge, and attitudes.

Purpose

In view of the variety of existing needs for consumer socialization research, this study examined the following different aspects of adolescent consumer learning that appeared to be of concern to the various interest groups.

1. It investigated the absolute and relative influences of mass media, family, and peers on the development of specific consumption-related values and motivations.

2. It examined the development of young people's capabilities to process information and evaluate marketing stimuli during adolescence.

3. It investigated the effects of existing consumer education materials and practices on the development of certain types of effective consumer behavior.

4. It tested and compared two general models of socialization—the cognitive developmental model and the social learning model—in explaining adolescent consumer socialization.

The study examined the development of specific consumption-related cognitions and behaviors (skills, knowledge, attitudes, and values) that appeared to have implications in terms of the issues for consumer socialization research. Consumer learning cognitions were classified into four categories on the basis of their level of cognitive complexity (simple vs. complex) and their relevance to the consumption behavior or transaction (direct vs. indirect).

The first category (direct-simple) included attitudes toward advertising, salespeople, prices, brands, and stores. The second category (indirect-simple) included basic knowledge about consumer affairs in the marketplace. The third category (direct-complex) included the ability to filter puffery in advertising, cognitively differentiate advertising stimuli, seek information from a variety of sources prior to decision making, and manage consumer finances. The fourth category (indirect-complex) included materialistic values and economic and social motivations for consumption. The consumption-related behaviors examined were those that contribute to the society's welfare, commonly referred to as "socially desirable consumer behavior"; they were referred to here as "consumer activism."

Research Approach

This study followed a rough existing blueprint outlining what a socialization theory should look like. Using the broad theoretical and conceptual notions of socialization in the specific context of consumer socialization, the development of consumption-related skills, knowledge, and attitudes were investigated as a function of three types of variables: (1) socialization processes derived from the social learning model of socialization, which were conceptualized in terms of the adolescent's interaction with four consumer socialization agents: family, mass media, peers, and school; (2) social class and sex, which served as social structural constraints that located the person in his social environment; and (3) maturational development indexed by the adolescent's age, a variable suggested by theories of cognitive development and psychological adjustment to one's environment.

A review of the research literature drawn from various theoretical and research perspectives (e.g, child psychology, consumer behavior, home economics, communication research) provided bases for formulating research hypotheses relevant to the development of consumption-related cognitions and behaviors of interest in this study. Of the several hypotheses formulated, *the main research or guiding hypotheses* were the following:

1. With respect to *the influence of the socialization agents*, it was postulated that:

a. *from mass media and peers*, adolescents learn "expressive" elements of consumption (e.g., materialism and social motivations).

b. *from parents*, adolescents learn basic "rational" aspects of consumption (e.g., budgeting skills).

c. *from school*, adolescents learn "socially desirable" behaviors and cognitions (e.g., consumer affairs knowledge).

2. With respect to the *effects of social structural variables* (social class and sex), it was expected that adolescents from low-income homes would have less experience with money and goods and, therefore, they would be less aware of their consumer environment than their counterparts from higher income homes.

3. With respect to the effects of *cognitive development*, significant differences were expected to be found among younger and older adolescents in the extent to which (a) adolescents in each group had acquired complex consumer skills and (b) adolescents had integrated simple and complex consumer skills.

The *sample* for this research study consisted of 806 adolescent respondents selected from 13 schools in 7 towns and cities in urban, suburban, semirural, and rural Wisconsin. Self-administered questionnaires were completed by respondents at middle schools and senior high schools. Attempts were made to include in the final sample adolescents representing adequate numbers of both sexes, age groups, geographical locations, and social classes.

Findings

With respect to the influence of *the four socialization agents* (mass media, family, peers, and school), the data presented in this study showed:

1. *Mass media* may be an important agent of adolescent consumer socialization. Various measures of media-adolescent interactions predicted several aspects of consumer learning, as follows:

a. Amount of *exposure to television* correlated positively with favorability of attitudes toward advertising and brands, materialistic attitudes, social motivations for consumption, and ability to cognitively differentiate advertising content in commercials. It correlated negatively with favorability of attitudes toward prices and economic motivations for consumption.

b. *Public affairs media use* was an important predictor of the amount of adolescent consumer affairs knowledge.

c. Amount of *newspaper readership* was an important correlate of favorable attitudes toward prices; consumer affairs knowledge; ability to cognitively filter puffery in advertising, differentiate advertising stimuli in commercials, manage consumer finances, and seek information prior to decision making; economic motivations for consumption; and socially desirable consumer acts. It correlated negatively with favorability of attitudes toward stores.

d. *Social utility reasons for watching television advertisements* was a strong predictor of the adolescent's favorability of attitudes toward advertising and brands, the strength of materialistic attitudes and social motivations for consumption, and the adolescent's ability to filter puffery in advertising.

e. *Social utility reasons for watching television programs* correlated positively with consumer affairs knowledge, materialistic attitudes, economic motivations for consumption, and the abilities to filter puffery in advertising and to seek information prior to making purchase decisions; it correlated negatively with favorability of attitudes toward brands.

Thus different consumer skills may be learned as a function of the amount, types, and uses of mass media by adolescents.

2. *Family* as a socialization agent appears to contribute relatively little to the adolescent's acquisition of the various consumer skills studied. Only socially desirable consumer behaviors and economic motivations for consumption appear to develop as a function of the amount of adolescents' interaction with their parents.

3. *Peers* may be an important agent of adolescent consumer socialization. Adolescents appear to learn the expressive aspects of consumption (materialistic attitudes and social motivations for consumption) from their peers. Interpersonal discussions with peers about consumer matters seem to lead to the formation of favorable attitudes toward advertising, a greater amount of consumer affairs knowledge, and the abilities to filter puffery in advertising and to seek information prior to decision making.

4. The *school* seems to be the least important agent of consumer socialization during adolescence. The number of consumer-related courses taken in school was a very weak predictor of the consumer skills examined in this research.

The findings of this research suggest that mass media and peers may be the most important sources of adolescents' consumer information shaping their consumption-related cognitions and behaviors. Adolescents appear to learn from these two socialization agents not only the "expressive" elements of consumption but also a wide variety of other skills, knowledge, attitudes, and values. Parents may be of secondary importance, whereas school apparently plays a very minor role in the adolescent's consumer socialization process.

The investigation of the effects of *social structural variables* (social class and sex) on adolescent consumer learning also revealed some interesting differences. The findings suggested that *social class* is an important antecedent variable in adolescent consumer socialization. Upper social class adolescents possessed the abilities to cognitively filter puffery in advertising, to differentiate advertising stimuli, and to manage consumer finances to a significantly greater extent than did lower social class adolescents. They also had more knowledge about consumer affairs and stronger economic motivations for consumption. These findings support the contention that the socioeconomic environment within which the child is brought up conditions the learning of this consumer environment.

Some *sex* differences also emerged. Male adolescents had stronger materialistic attitudes and social motivations for consumption, more favorable attitudes toward stores, and a greater amount of consumer affairs knowledge than did female adolescents. Female respondents, however, showed more favorable attitudes toward advertising, had a greater ability to cognitively differentiate advertising stimuli, and seemed to be performing more socially desirable consumer behaviors than the male adolescents.

Lastly, the adolescent's cognitive development (indexed by his age) was examined as a predictor of several consumption-related skills, knowledge, and attitudes. *Age* correlated positively with the strength of favorable attitudes toward stores, amount of consumer affairs knowledge, degree of cognitive differentiation of advertising stimuli, ability to seek information prior to purchasing products and to manage consumer finances, economic motivations for consumption, and consumer activism. It correlated negatively with the favorability of attitudes toward advertising, brands, and prices.

Although these skills appeared to be developing concomitantly with age, the cognitive developmental model of socialization, which suggests that socialization takes place by the age of 15, did not offer a satisfactory explanation of adolescent consumer socialization. The findings of this study suggest that adolescents continue to develop and integrate their consumption-related skills, knowledge, and attitudes during late adolescence (past the age of 15). These findings lead to the conclusion that consumer socialization appears to be more of a social learning process than a psychological adjustment to one's environment.

Implications

Several findings in this study were based on theoretical notions, i.e., hypotheses were generated based on previous work in disciplinary areas. Other findings were empirical in nature and can be used to formulate new hypotheses, to modify existing theories, and to guide research efforts in this area. Regardless of the nature of the findings, that is, whether they derive from theoretical formulations or are purely descriptive in nature, they do appear to provide information with important implications for marketing practitioners, public policy makers, consumer educators, and students of socialization and consumer behavior.

Implications for Marketers

The marketing implications of the research findings can be grouped into two categories: implications with respect to marketing strategy formulation and implications with respect to the critics' attacks on marketing practices directed at young people.

In formulating marketing strategy, marketers should keep in mind that youth in different socioeconomic spectra of society have different motivations for consumption. This study found that adolescents in higher social classes had greater economic motivations for consumption than adolescents in lower social classes. Thus, for example, marketing communications stressing the economic or functional aspects of a product would be more likely to be received favorably by adolescents in upper social classes than by adolescents in lower social classes.

Marketers might also do well to coordinate their marketing communications according to the *age* of the adolescent consumers. For example, comparative advertising (i.e., advertising stressing differences in attributes among products or brands) is more likely to be effective among older adolescents than younger adolescents, because the older group is more likely to cognitively differentiate and recall such advertising content. This is not to say that no comparative advertising is effective for younger teen-agers.

In this study the younger adolescents had more favorable attitudes toward prices than did older adolescents. The latter group had more favorable attitudes toward brands than their younger counterparts. These findings suggest that the importance of product attributes considered in decision making varies with age, and consequently marketers would do well to isolate the significant product attributes used in decision making by different age groups of youth.

Furthermore, adolescents appear to resist advertising more with age in the form of greater cognitive and attitudinal defenses (e.g., less favorable attitudes toward advertising and its purposes). Therefore, it would seem more difficult to communicate through advertising with older adolescents than with younger adolescents. Perhaps marketers would be more successful if they tried to reach older adolescents through informal groups, for example, by stimulating interpersonal discussions of their products through advertising. As the results of this study indicate, informal group influence appears to become significant with age.

Marketers also should keep in mind the *sex* of the youth market with which they are trying to communicate. The content of the message should reflect the sex composition of the market. The expressive aspects of consumption appear to be more relevant to male than to female adolescents. Similarly, female adolescents appear to retain product-attribute information to a greater extent than do their male counterparts, and they might be more receptive to comparative advertising.

Marketers can use some of the findings from this study to respond to charges made by advertising critics about the effects of advertising on young people. Although many critics argue that advertising results in the development of materialistic orientations and nonrational consumer behavior among young people, this study showed that social processes may condition the young people's perception of the importance of the expressive and materialistic aspects of consumption, motivating them to pay attention to advertising and programming content. Such attention in turn seems to contribute to the development of materialistic attitudes and social (nonrational) motivations for consumption. Thus marketers could argue that interpersonal social processes, the origins of which are not yet known, are necessary for learning such motivations and cognitions.

Implications for Public Policy Makers

Policy makers are concerned with the socialization of young people and the processes leading to undesirable consumer socialization as well as to socially desirable consumer acts. This study indicates that young people may be susceptible to advertising at least through early adolescence. Their cognitive resistance to advertising does not seem to develop prior to high school years.

Advertising that might be inherently undesirable appears to be that which emphasizes the social significance and uses of products and services. Young people who tend to watch advertising for social utility reasons seem to learn the expressive aspects of consumption at the expense of the economic or "rational" motivations. This kind of viewing may be contributing to the development of brand "loyalties." Watching television advertising for social utility reasons also may be weakening the adolescent's ability to filter puffery in advertising. Whereas social interpersonal processes (e.g., communication with peers) might cause the youth to view television commercials for social utility reasons, the mere *availability* and *demonstrations* of social uses of products in advertisements would appear to *contribute* to the formation of materialistic attitudes and to social, nonrational motivations for consumption.

The amount of television viewing also may be contributing to the strength of materialistic attitudes and social motivations for consumption. Such learning may be the effect of programming and/or advertising. At least for the development of social motivations for consumption, programming effects may be minimal; they are more likely to shape the person's attitudes toward materialism along with other socially desirable consumer skills, such as economic motivations for consumption, ability to filter puffery in advertising, information seeking, and consumer affairs knowledge.

Implications for Consumer Educators

The results of this study provide some useful guidelines for the development of adult and adolescent consumer education curricula. Adult consumer education materials should include information on aspects of the consumer role that adolescents do not appear to learn at home or at school. Knowledge about consumer affairs and the abilities to manage consumer finances and to seek information from various sources prior to decision making are skills that parents should emphasize at home.

Consumer education materials and practices designed to teach adolescents how to be effective consumers should emphasize (1) socially desirable consumer acts (e.g., comparison shopping), (2) economic or rational aspects of the consumer decision-making process, (3) use of certain sources of consumer information, (4) knowledge about consumer legal rights and business terms in the marketplace, and (5) skills for budgeting and managing consumer finances.

Consumer educators also should know that the need for consumer education in school appears to exist among adolescents from lower socioeconomic families. Furthermore, male adolescents appear to lag behind female adolescents on the performance of socially desirable consumer behaviors, whereas female adolescents to a greater extent than male adolescents need to be provided with information that would increase their knowledge about consumer matters.

Implications for Socialization Theory

The findings of this study suggest that consumer socialization appears to take place throughout adolescence. The mere cognitive development of the child's ability to understand consumption-related stimuli does not appear to be a sufficient condition for consumer learning. Consumer socialization seems to be explained by theories of social learning, which suggest that socialization takes place during the person's interaction with socialization agents. Thus, even if the person is mature enough to understand his commercial environment, consumption-related skills, knowledge, and attitudes may not develop in the absence of the person's interaction with various agents that appear to condition the person's perception of his consumer environment and thus cause him to learn by making this environment of greater relevance to him.

Directions for Future Research

The results of this study suggest several directions that might be taken in future research. Perhaps one of the most demanding needs for research is understanding the development of social motivations for using the mass media. This research suggests that the learning of expressive elements of consumption may be mainly a function of social utility reasons for watching television programs and advertisements. However, *how* such motivations develop is not quite clear. It would be interesting to know whether social reasons for media use could develop as a function of the child's interaction with the various socialization agents (especially with family and peers) or whether these processes develop as a function of specific social and cultural characteristics, as some research suggests.[1]

Another subject for additional research is the nature of the family environment in which the adolescent is brought up. Factors such as availability of opportunities for consumer learning and other structural variables may affect the acquisition of specific skills. This study, for example, found social class to be an important variable affecting consumer-learning skills. It would be useful to know whether the better consumer learning taking place among adolescents of higher socioeconomic class is due to various socialization practices among these families or to structural factors such as availability of newspaper and magazines in these homes.

The findings of this study suggest that learning processes apparently vary by age of the adolescent consumer. It would be useful to know the effectiveness of various learning processes and socialization agents in teaching different consumer skills to adolescents at various ages. Such information could have public policy implications for controlling processes leading to socially desirable consumer acts (e.g., designing student consumer education curricula and educating adult consumers on how they should attempt to train their children at home). Future research could examine the reason(s) for failure to learn at school. The data in this study could not answer questions regarding the low correlations found between, for example, the number of consumer-related courses taken at school and the amount of consumer affairs knowledge. Studies in this area could examine the effects of present consumer education materials and practices under carefully controlled experimental conditions.

This research was concerned mainly with the short-term effects of socialization agents on the acquisition of consumer skills. It is possible that certain kinds of interactions with socialization agents (e.g., media) and experiences during early adolescence could have long-term effects on adolescent consumer learning.[2] Longitudinal research could probably best answer questions concerning long-term effects of socialization agents and earlier learning on adolescent consumer socialization.

Finally, it is possible that consumer socialization might continue throughout the individual's life.[3] Knowledge of the kinds of skills that might be learned and how well these are learned throughout the person's life cycle as a result of changes in life-styles (e.g., marriage, retirement) might have significant implications for public policy formulation and adult consumer education.

---

1. See, for example, D.B. Kandel and G.S. Lesser, *Youth in Two Worlds* (San Francisco: Jossey-Bass, Inc., 1972); F.M. Katz, "The Meaning of Success: Some Differences in Value Systems of Social Classes," *Journal of Social Psychology*, February 1964, pp. 141-148; and M.H. Kuhn, "Factors in Personality: Socio-Cultural Determinants as Seen Through the Amish," in F.L.K. Hsu, ed., *Aspects of Culture and Personality* (New York, Abelard-Schuman, Inc., 1954).

2. Scott Ward, "Consumer Socialization," *Journal of Consumer Research*, September 1974, pp. 1-14.

3. Orville G. Brim and G. Wheller, *Socialization After Childhood: Two Essays* (New York: John Wiley & Sons, Inc., 1966).

Appendix A
Consumer Questionnaire

Instructions

You are being asked to fill out this questionnaire to help us find out what students know about consumer matters. *This is not a test and you won't be graded on your replies.* Answer each question as honestly as you can, but if you are not sure about a particular answer check or write the answer that comes *closest* to what you think you know.

If you don't understand a question or the directions, raise your hand and someone will help you.

Take as much time as you need and *BE SURE TO ANSWER EVERY QUESTION.*

Do not pay attention to the numbers you see in parentheses or elsewhere in the questionnaire; they are included only to assist us in processing your answers.

YOU MAY BEGIN NOW. DON'T STOP UNTIL YOU HAVE ANSWERED ALL THE QUESTIONS.

(1-7)

1. For each of the following, check whether you think it is *True, False,* or you
Don't Know.   (8-18)

	True	False	Don't Know
	3	2	1

a. When you buy stock you own part of a company.

b. Milk sold in the store must show the last day it can be sold.

c. A "shortage economy" is when the country is short of money.

d. The mortgage is the down payment on a house.

e. When you have liability insurance you don't have to pay for wrecking someone else's car.

f. The Better Business Bureau helps consumers, not merchants.

g. A credit union is a group of people who agree to save their money together and make loans to each other.

h. Ground beef sold at the store must have two prices, one that shows how much the whole package costs and another that says how much one pound costs.

i. All products show the name of the company that makes them.

j. It is legal for a store to advertise a product at $20.00 and sell it for $21.00 on the same day.

k. The Office of Consumer Protection helps people who have been tricked by merchants.

2a. Write the *number* of courses you have taken or are taking in each of the
following areas.   (19-23)

Number of Courses

Consumer education _____

Home economics _____

Economics _____

Environmental science _____

Guidance (Job Education) _____

2b. Write the names of any other courses you have taken in which you have studied about consumer matters.   (24)

_____

3. For each of the following, check whether you do it *quite a lot, sometimes, rarely, never,* or *don't know.*   (25-31)

	Quite a lot	Sometimes	Rarely	Never	Don't Know
	5	4	3	2	1
a. I keep track of the money I spend and save.	_____	_____	_____	_____	_____
b. I plan how to spend my money.	_____	_____	_____	_____	_____
c. I shop around before buying something that costs a lot of money.	_____	_____	_____	_____	_____
d. I carefully read *most* of the things they write on packages or labels.	_____	_____	_____	_____	_____
e. I compare prices and brands before buying something that costs a lot of money.	_____	_____	_____	_____	_____
f. I try to buy returnable bottles instead of disposable ones.	_____	_____	_____	_____	_____
g. I make sure that the lights and TV set at home are off when they are not being used.	_____	_____	_____	_____	_____

4. About how much time do you spend doing the following on an *average school day*?

a. Watching television	Hours _____	Minutes _____	(32-34)
b. Listening to the radio	Hours _____	Minutes _____	(35-37)
c. Reading newspapers	Hours _____	Minutes _____	(38-40)
d. Reading magazines	Hours _____	Minutes _____	(41-43)

5. About how often do you read the following things in the newspapers?   (44-48)

	Every day	Several times a week	Once or twice a week	Less than once a week	Never
	5	4	3	2	1
The Comics	___	___	___	___	___
Sports	___	___	___	___	___
News about the government and politics	___	___	___	___	___
News about the economy	___	___	___	___	___
Advertisements	___	___	___	___	___

6. About how often do you watch the following on television?   (49-55)

	Every day	Several times a week	Once or twice a week	Less than once a week	Never
	5	4	3	2	1
National or local news	___	___	___	___	___
Sport events	___	___	___	___	___
Movies	___	___	___	___	___
Variety shows (Sonny & Cher, Donny & Marie, etc.)	___	___	___	___	___
Cartoons	___	___	___	___	___
Police and adventure shows	___	___	___	___	___
Comedy shows	___	___	___	___	___

7. Below are some things that have been said on television. For each one check whether you believe it is *completely true, partly true,* or *not true at all.*   (56-67)

	Believe it is completely true	Believe it is partly true	Believe it is not true at all
	3	2	1
a. Chevrolet's engine guarantee is for 60,000 miles or 5 years.	___	___	___

b. State Farm is all you need to know about insurance. _____ _____ _____

c. Honda Civic gets 43 miles per gallon on the highway. _____ _____ _____

d. Arm & Arm—the first spray deodorant with baking soda. _____ _____ _____

e. The American breakfast, no mistake, starts with sugar, milk, and Kellogg's corn flakes. _____ _____ _____

f. Amana—the greatest cooking discovery since fire. _____ _____ _____

g. Bayer works wonders. _____ _____ _____

h. Sanka is 97% caffeine-free coffee. _____ _____ _____

i. Mr. Coffee—the fastest American coffee maker. _____ _____ _____

j. Brylcream makes success go to your head. _____ _____ _____

k. Presto cooks a hamburger in 60 seconds. _____ _____ _____

l. Ultra Brite can help your love life. _____ _____ _____

8. For each of the following statements, check whether you *strongly agree, somewhat agree, don't know, somewhat disagree,* or *strongly disagree.*   (68-73)

	Strongly agree	Somewhat agree	Don't know	Somewhat disagree	Strongly disagree
	5	4	3	2	1
a. It is really true that money can buy happiness.	_____	_____	_____	_____	_____
b. My dream in life is to be able to own expensive things.	_____	_____	_____	_____	_____
c. People judge others by the things they own.	_____	_____	_____	_____	_____
d. I buy some things that I secretly hope will impress other people.	_____	_____	_____	_____	_____

e. Money is the most
important thing to consider
in choosing a job.   _____ _____ _____ _____ _____

f. I think others judge me as a
person by the kinds of
products and brands I use.   _____ _____ _____ _____ _____

9. Following is a list of sentences* about products you may have heard or seen in advertisements. Carefully go over each sentence and fill in as many blanks as you can with the right product name. (Example: _Magnavox_ TV automatically adjusts its screen to the light of the room.)   (74-75)

a. _____ makes 0 to 50 miles in 8.2 seconds.

b. _____ is more effective in helping stop wetness than any leading brand.

c. _____ penetrates deeper than most nasal sprays.

d. _____ TV has the best picture and fewer repairs.

e. _____ camera weighs 16 ounces and costs $66.00.

f. _____ , the candy mint with retsyn.

g. _____ , the TV network of the Olympic games.

h. _____ , the natural pH balance shampoo.

i. _____ , the astronauts' drink.

j. _____ , the toothpaste with baking soda.

k. _____ , the soap with cocoa butter and moisturizers.

l. When you catch a cold you take one _____ capsule every twelve hours.

10. Following are some ideas about advertising, products, stores, and salespeople. For each statement check whether you *strongly agree, somewhat agree, don't know, somewhat disagree*, or *strongly disagree*.   (8-43)

	Strongly agree	Somewhat agree	Don't know	Somewhat disagree	Strongly disagree
	5	4	3	2	1
a. Advertising makes people buy things they don't really need.	_____	_____	_____	_____	_____
b. Advertised brands are better than those not advertised.	_____	_____	_____	_____	_____

c. Quality products are made
only by well-known
companies. _____ _____ _____ _____ _____

d. Most television commercials
are fun to watch. _____ _____ _____ _____ _____

e. I like to try new and
different brands. _____ _____ _____ _____ _____

f. Once I have made a choice
on which store to buy things
from, I prefer shopping there
without trying other stores. _____ _____ _____ _____ _____

g. When I see or hear something new advertised, I
often want to buy it. _____ _____ _____ _____ _____

h. I prefer a certain brand of
most products I buy or use. _____ _____ _____ _____ _____

i. Many products are not
worth the price you pay for
them. _____ _____ _____ _____ _____

j. Advertisements help people
buy things that are best for
them. _____ _____ _____ _____ _____

k. Well-known stores never sell
poor quality products. _____ _____ _____ _____ _____

l. Most salespeople try to
trick you into buying some-
thing you don't really need. _____ _____ _____ _____ _____

m. Most advertising that comes
through the mail is junk
and not worth looking at. _____ _____ _____ _____ _____

n. Many brand names of
products on the market are
of poor quality. _____ _____ _____ _____ _____

o. Products on sale are always
a bargain. _____ _____ _____ _____ _____

p. I would buy most products
I use from any store that
sells them. _____ _____ _____ _____ _____

q. Most radio commercials are
annoying. _____ _____ _____ _____ _____

r. Most products sold at reduced price are of poor quality.

s. Salespeople are honest.

t. I think there should be less advertising than there is now.

u. Most products sold at reduced price are never really on sale at all.

v. Salespeople help you buy those things that are best for you.

w. Most magazine advertisements are enjoyable to look at.

x. I don't care about the brand names of most products I buy.

y. Salespeople are friendly.

z. I prefer doing most of my shopping in the same stores I have always shopped in.

aa. Most advertisements tell the truth.

bb. Brand-name products work better than "off brands."

cc. Most products are sold at reduced prices because they are too old.

dd. Most salespeople take advantage of those who don't know much about buying things.

ee. I don't pay much attention to advertising.

ff. You always have to pay a bit more for the best.

gg. I judge the value of some products by the name of the store that sells them.

hh. Salespeople are polite.

ii. Most newspaper advertisements are enjoyable to
look at.

jj. I like to know the price of
everything.

11. Below are some things people your age may buy. For each one check those
people or places you would *rely on most* for information or advice *before buying*.
(YOU MAY CHECK MORE THAN ONE ANSWER IN EACH ROW.)

	Friends	TV ads	Sales persons	Consumer reports	One or both of my parents	Newspaper or magazine ads	
a. Camera							(44-49)
b. Hair dryer							(50-55)
c. Pocket calculator							(56-61)
d. Bicycle							(62-67)
e. Wrist watch							(68-73)

(1-7)

12. Now we want you to tell us whether the things on the following list are
important to know before buying five different products. For each item that you
read on the list check *whether YOU think it is important to know before buying a
bicycle, a watch, a camera, a pocket calculator,* or *a hair dryer. (FOR EACH
ITEM THAT YOU READ YOU MAY CHECK AS MANY PRODUCTS AS YOU
WANT OR NONE OF THE PRODUCTS.)*

Before buying a	Bicycle	Watch	Camera	Pocket calculator	Hair dryer	
It is important to know:						
a. What friends think of different brands or products.						(8-12)
b. Guarantees on different brands.						(13-17)
c. What kinds of people buy certain brands or products.						(18-22)
d. The name of the company that makes the product.						(23-27)
e. Whether any brands are on sale.						(28-32)

f. What others think of
people who use
certain brands or
products. _____ _____ _____ _____ _____ (33-37)

g. Kinds of materials
different brands
are made of. _____ _____ _____ _____ _____ (38-42)

h. What brands or
products to buy to
make good impres-
sions on others. _____ _____ _____ _____ _____ (43-47)

i. Quality of the store
selling a particular
brand. _____ _____ _____ _____ _____ (48-52)

13. Check whether each of the following happens *very often, often, sometimes, rarely*, or *never*.
(53-70)

	Very often	Often	Sometimes	Rarely	Never
	5	4	3	2	1
a. My parents tell me what things I should or shouldn't buy.					
b. I ask my friends for advice about buying things.					
c. My parents want to know what I do with my money.					
d. I help my parents buy things for the family.					
e. My friends and I talk about buying things.					
f. My parents complain when they don't like something I bought for myself.					
g. My parents ask me what I think about things they buy for themselves.					
h. My friends and I talk about things we see or hear advertised.					

i. My parents and I talk
about things we see or
hear advertised. ___ ___ ___ ___ ___

j. I ask my parents for
advice about buying
things. ___ ___ ___ ___ ___

k. My parents tell me why
they buy some things
for themselves. ___ ___ ___ ___ ___

l. My friends ask me for
advice about buying
things. ___ ___ ___ ___ ___

m. I go shopping with my
parents. ___ ___ ___ ___ ___

n. My friends tell me what
things I should or
shouldn't buy. ___ ___ ___ ___ ___

o. My parents and I talk
about buying things. ___ ___ ___ ___ ___

p. My parents tell me I
should decide about
things I should or
shouldn't buy. ___ ___ ___ ___ ___

q. I go shopping with my
friends. ___ ___ ___ ___ ___

r. My parents tell me what
they do with their
money. ___ ___ ___ ___ ___

14. Following are some reasons people watch TV shows and TV commercials. For
each reason, check whether you *ever watch TV shows, TV commercials, neither,*
or *don't know. (You may check both TV shows and TV commercials.)*   (8-47)

	I watch TV shows	I watch TV commercials	Neither	Don't know
a. To get ideas on how to be successful.	___	___	___	___ (8-11)
b. To find out what kinds of people use certain products.	___	___	___	___ (12-15)
c. To find out what kinds of products to buy to feel like those people I wish I were.	___	___	___	___ (16-19)

d. To learn what things to
   buy to make good
   impressions on others. _____ _____ _____ _____ (20-23)

e. To dream of the good
   life. _____ _____ _____ _____ (24-27)

f. To find out what
   qualities people like in
   others. _____ _____ _____ _____ (28-31)

g. To find out how others
   solve the same problems
   I have. _____ _____ _____ _____ (32-35)

h. To give me something
   to talk about with
   others. _____ _____ _____ _____ (36-39)

i. To learn about the "in"
   things to buy. _____ _____ _____ _____ (40-43)

j. To tell others something
   they don't already know
   about new ideas or
   products. _____ _____ _____ _____ (44-47)

15. How old are you? _____   16. What grade are you in? _____ (48-51)

17a. What does your father do for a living? _____

17b. Where does your father work? _____ (52-53)

18a. What does your mother do for a living? _____

18b. Where does your mother work? _____ (54-55)

19. What is your sex?   Male _____   Female _____   (56)

20. About how much money do you earn in a week during the school year?
    $ _____ (57-60)

21. About how much of your own money do you usually spend in a week?
    $ _____ (61-64)

22. About how much money do you get weekly from?   Work $ _____
    Allowance $ _____ (65-67)

23. How many brothers do you have? ____ What are their ages? ____ (68-70)

24. How many sisters do you have? ____ What are their ages? ____ (71-73)

25. Write *about how much* money YOU THINK the *AVERAGE AMERICAN FAMILY* with two children and a total monthly income of $1,000 spends on each expense item of the following budget.

The average American family spends a month about:

a. $ _____ for *food*. (74)

b. $ _____ for *clothes*. (75)

c. $ _____ for *home expenses*, like house payments, upkeep, and repairs. (76)

d. $ _____ for *automobile expenses* (one car), like payments, maintenance, and gas. (77)

e. $ _____ for *other expenses*, like recreation and personal care items. (78)

f. $ _____ for *savings* (money to put aside). (79)

  $ 1,000 TOTAL (80)

Bibliography

Action for Children's Television. Testimony before the Federal Trade Commission, November 10, 1971.

Alexander, K.S. "Some Aspects of Sex Differences in Relation to Marketing." *Journal of Marketing*, July 1947, pp. 158-172.

Bandura, Albert. "Modeling Influences on Children." Testimony to the Federal Trade Commission, November 1971.

Banks, Seymour. Testimony before the Federal Trade Commission, October 28, 1971.

Bauer, Raymond A. "The Initiative of the Audience." *Journal of Advertising Research*, June 1963, pp. 2-7.

Bauer, Raymond A. "The Obstinate Audience: The Influence Process from the Point of View of Social Communication." *American Psychologist*, May 1964, pp. 319-328.

Bauer, Raymond A. and Greyser, Stephen. *Advertising in America: The Consumer View*. Boston: Harvard Business School, Division of Research, 1968.

Blatt, Joan; Spencer, Lyle; and Ward, Scott. "A Cognitive Development Study of Children's Reactions to Television Advertising." In *Television and Social Behavior, IV: Television in Day to Day Use: Patterns of Use*, edited by Eli A. Rubinstein, George H. Comstock, and John P. Murray. Washington, D.C.: U.S. Government Printing Office, 1971.

Bloom, Paul N. and Silver, Mark J. "Consumer Education: Marketers Take Heed." *Harvard Business Review*, January-February 1976, pp. 32-42, 149-150.

Brim, Orville G. "Socialization through the Life Cycle." In *Socialization After Childhood*, edited by O. Brim and S. Wheeler. New York: John Wiley & Sons, Inc., 1966, pp. 3-49.

Campbell, Earnest Q. "Adolescent Socialization." In *Handbook of Socialization Theory and Research*, edited by David A. Goslin. Chicago: Rand McNally, 1969.

Cannon, Kenneth C.; Staples, Ruth; and Carlson, Irene. "Personal Appearance as a Factor in Personal Acceptance." *Journal of Home Economics*, November 1952, pp. 710-713.

Cateora, Philip R. *An Analysis of the Teen-age Market*. Austin, Texas: Bureau of Business Research, University of Texas, 1963.

Chaffee, Steven H.; McLeod, Jack M.; and Atkin, Charles K. "Parental Influences on Adolescent Media Use." *American Behavioral Scientist*, January-February 1971, pp. 323-340.

Chaffee, Steven H.; McLeod, Jack M.; and Wackman, Daniel B. "Family Communication Patterns and Adolescent Political Participation." In *Explorations of Political Socialization*, edited by J. Dennis. New York: John Wiley & Sons, Inc., 1972.

Diamond, S.L. "Consumer Education: Perspectives on the State of the Art." Mimeographed. Cambridge, Massachusetts: Harvard University, Graduate School of Business Administration, 1974.

Duncan, Otis D. *Introduction to Structural Equation Models*. New York: Academic Press, 1975.

Duncan, Otis D. "A Socioeconomic Index for All Occupations." In *Occupations and Social Status*, edited by Albert J. Reiss, Jr. New York: Free Press, 1961.

Engel, James F.; Blackwell, Roger D.; and Kollat, David T. *Consumer Behavior*. 2nd ed. Hinsdale, Illinois: The Dryden Press, 1973.

Fisk, George. "Criteria for a Theory of Responsible Consumption." *Journal of Marketing*, January 1973, pp. 24-31.

Gagné, Robert M. "Contributions of Learning to Human Development." In *Human Development and Cognitive Processes*, edited by John Eliot. New York: Holt, Rinehart and Winston, Inc., 1971, pp. 111-128.

Gavian, Ruth W. and Nanassy, Louis C. "Economic Competence as a Goal of Elementary School Education." *Elementary School Journal*, January 1955, pp. 270-273.

"Getting Across to the Youth." *Business Week*, October 18, 1969, pp. 89-90.

Gilkison, Paul. "Teen-agers' Perceptions of Buying Frame of Reference: A Decade of Retrospect." *Journal of Retailing*, Summer 1973, pp. 25-37.

Ginsburg, Herbert and Opper, Sylvia. *Piaget's Theory of Intellectual Development*. Englewood Cliffs, New Jersey: Prentice-Hall, 1969.

Goslin, D.A., ed. *Handbook of Socialization Theory and Research*. Chicago: Rand McNally and Co., 1969.

Granbois, Donald H. "The Role of Communication in the Family Decision Making Process." In *Toward Scientific Marketing*, edited by Stephen A. Greyser. Chicago: American Marketing Association, 1964.

Guest, Lester P. "Brand Loyalty: Twelve Years Later." *Journal of Applied Psychology*, December 1955, pp. 405-408.

Guest, Lester P. "The Genesis of Brand Awareness." *Journal of Applied Psychology*, December 1942, pp. 800-808.

Hamilton, Janice and Warden, Jessie. "Student's Role in a High School Community and His Clothing Behavior." *Journal of Home Economics*, December 1966, pp. 781-791.

Hanushek, Eric A. and Jackson, John E. *Statistical Methods for Social Scientists*. New York: Academic Press, 1977.

Hawkins, Calvin H. "A Study of the Use of Consumer Education Concepts by High School Graduates." *Journal of Consumer Affairs*, Summer 1977, pp. 122-127.

Hess, R.D. "Social Class and Ethnic Influences on Socialization." In *Manual of Child Psychology*, edited by Paul H. Mussey, vol. 2, 3rd ed. New York: John Wiley & Sons, Inc., 1970, pp. 457-459.

Hoerl, Arthur and Kennard, Robert. "Ridge Regression: Biased Estimation for Nonorthogonal Problems." *Technometrics*, February 1970, pp. 55-67.

Horn, Thomas D. and Miller, Lebery. "Children's Concepts Regarding Debt." *Elementary School Journal*, March 1955, pp. 406-412.

James, Don L. *Youth, Media, and Advertising*. Austin, Texas: Bureau of Business Research, University of Texas, 1971.

Janis, I.L. and Field, P.B. "Sex Differences and Personality." In *Personality and Persuasibility*, edited by C. Hovland and I. Janis. New Haven, Connecticut: Yale University Press, 1955, pp. 55-68.

Jennings, Kent M. and Niemi, Richard G. "Patterns of Political Learning." *Harvard Educational Review*, Summer 1968, pp. 443-467.

Kagan, Jerome. "The Child in the Family." In *Daedalus*, American Academy of Arts and Sciences, Spring 1977, pp. 33-56.

Kandel, D.B. and Lesser, G.S. *Youth in Two Worlds*. San Francisco: Jossey-Bass, Inc., 1972.

Katz, Elihu; Blumler, Jay C.; and Gurevitch, Michael. "Utilization of Mass Communication by the Individual." In *The Uses of Mass Communications*, edited by J.C. Blumler and E. Katz. Beverly Hills, California: Sage Publications, 1974.

Katz, F.M. "The Meaning of Success: Some Differences in Value Systems of Social Classes." *Journal of Social Psychology*, February 1964, pp. 141-148.

Keiser, Stephen K. "Awareness of Brands and Slogans." *Journal of Advertising Research*, August 1975, pp. 37-43.

Klapper, Joseph T. *The Effects of Mass Communication*. New York: Free Press, 1960.

Kohlberg, Lawrence. "The Cognitive Developmental Approach to Socialization." In *Handbook of Socialization Theory and Research*, edited by D.A. Goslin. Chicago: Rand McNally and Co., 1969.

Kuhn, M.H. "Factors of Personality: Socio-Cultural Determinants as Seen Through The Amish." In *Aspects of Culture and Personality*, edited by F.L.K. Hsu. New York: Abelard-Schuman, Inc., 1954.

Langrehr, F.W. and Mason, J.B. "The Development and Implementation of the Concept of Consumer Education." *Journal of Consumer Affairs*, Winter 1977, pp. 63-79.

Marshall, H.R. and Magrueder, Lucille. "Relations Between Parent Money Education Practices and Children's Knowledge and Use of Money." *Child Development*, vol. 31, 1960, pp. 253-284.

McLeod, Jack M. and Becker, Lee B. "Testing the Validity of Media Gratifications Through Political Effects Analysis." In *The Uses of Mass Communications*, edited by J.C. Blumler and E. Katz. Beverly Hills, California: Sage Publications, 1974.

McLeod, Jack M. and O'Keefe, Garret J., Jr. "The Socialization Prospective and Communication Behavior." In *Current Perspectives in Mass Communication Research*, edited by G. Kline and P. Tichenor. Beverly Hills, California: Sage Publications, 1972.

McNeal, James V. *Children as Consumers*. Marketing Study Series No. 9. Austin, Texas: Bureau of Business Research, University of Texas, 1964.

Millson, C.A. "Conformity to Peers Versus Adults in Early Adolescence." Doctoral Dissertation. New York: Cornell University, 1966.

Moore, Bernice M. and Holtzman, Wayne H. *Tomorrow's Parents: A Study of Youth and Their Families*. Austin, Texas: University of Texas Press, 1965.

Moore, Roy L. and Moschis, George P. "Teenagers' Reactions to Advertising." *Journal of Advertising*, forthcoming.

Moore, Roy L. and Stephens, Lowndes F. "Some Communication and Demographic Determinants of Adolescent Consumer Learning." *Journal of Consumer Research*, September 1975, pp. 80-92.

Moore, Roy L.; Moschis, George P.; and Stephens, Lowndes F. "An Exploratory Study of Consumer Role Perceptions in Adolescent Consumer Socialization." Paper presented to the International Communication Association, Chicago, April 1975.

Moschis, George P. and Churchill, Gilbert A., Jr. "Consumer Socialization: A Theoretical and Empirical Analysis." *Journal of Marketing Research*, forthcoming.

Moschis, George P. and Moore, Roy L. "An Analysis of the Acquisition of Some Consumer Competencies Among Adolescents." *Journal of Consumer Affairs*, forthcoming.

Moschis, George P.; Moore, Roy L.; and Stephens, Lowndes F. "Purchasing Patterns of Adolescent Consumers," *Journal of Retailing*, Spring 1977, pp. 17-26.

North Central Research Committee NC-24. *Adolescent Girls' Skirts, Part I: Mothers' and Daughters' Opinion of School Skirts.* Station Bulletin 478, NCR Research Pub-169. St. Paul: Agricultural Experiment Station, University of Minnesota, 1965.

Nunnally, Jum C. *Psychometric Theory.* New York: McGraw-Hill Company, Inc., 1967.

Parsons, T.; Bales, R.F.; and Shils, E.A. *Working Papers in the Theory of Action.* Glencoe, Illinois: The Free Press, 1953.

Phelan, Gladys K. and Schvaneveldt, Jay D. "Spending and Saving Patterns of Adolescent Siblings." *Journal of Home Economics,* February 1969, pp. 104-109.

Piaget, Jean. "The General Problems of the Psychological Development of the Child." In *Discussions on Child Development: Proceedings of the World Health Organization Study Group on the Psychological Development of the Child:IV,* edited by J.M. Tanner and B. Elders. New York: International Universities Press, 1960.

Preston, Ivan L. and Johnson, Ralph. "Puffery—A Problem the FTC Didn't Want (and May Try to Eliminate)." *Journalism Quarterly,* Autumn 1972, pp. 558-568.

Riesman, David; Glazer, Nathan; and Denny, Renel. *The Lonely Crowd.* New Haven, Connecticut: Yale University Press, 1950.

Riesman, David and Roseborough, Howard. "Careers and Consumer Behavior." In *Consumer Behavior, The Life Cycle and Consumer Behavior,* vol. 2, edited by Lincoln Clark. New York: New York University Press, 1955.

Robertson, Thomas S. "The Impact of Television Advertising on Children." *Wharton Quarterly,* Summer 1972, pp. 38-41.

Robertson, Thomas S. "Low-Commitment Consumer Behavior." *Journal of Advertising Research,* April 1976, pp. 19-24.

Rossiter, John R. and Robertson, Thomas S. "Children's TV Commercials: Testing for Defenses." *Journal of Communication,* Autumn 1974, pp. 137-144.

Rothschild, Michael L. "Involvement as a Determinant of Decision Making Styles." *Proceedings.* Chicago: American Marketing Association, 1975.

Sanders, Josephine R.; Salmi, A. Coskum; and Tozier, Enid F. "Congruence and Conflict in Buying Decisions of Mothers and Daughters." *Journal of Retailing,* Fall 1973, pp. 3-18.

Schiele, G.W. "How to Reach the Young Consumer." *Harvard Business Review,* March-April 1974, pp. 77-86.

Schnapper, Eric. "Consumer Legislation and the Poor." *The Yale Law Journal,* 1971, pp. 745-768.

Schramm, Wilbur; Lyle, Jack; and Parker, Edwin B. *Television in the Lives of Our Children.* Stanford, California: Stanford University Press, 1961.

Secord, Paul and Backman, Carl W. *Social Psychology*. New York: McGraw-Hill, 1964.

Steiner, Gary A. "The People Look at Television." *Journal of Business*, April 1963, pp. 272-304.

Thompson, Glen W. "Children's Acceptance of Television Advertising and the Relation of Television to School Achievement." *Journal of Educational Research*, December 1964, pp. 171-174.

Uhl, J.N. "Consumer Education and Protection." In *Economics of Consumer Protection*, edited by L.L. Mather. Danville, Illinois: The Interstate Printers and Publishers, Inc., 1971, pp. 11-21.

U.S. Bureau of Labor Statistics. *Monthly Labor Review*, July 1974, p. 39.

Vener, Arthur M. and Hoffer, Charles R. *Adolescent Orientation to Clothing*. Technical Bulletin 270. East Lansing, Michigan: Agricultural Experiment Station, Michigan State University, 1959.

Wackman, Daniel B.; McLeod, Jack M.; and Chaffee, Steven H. "Family Communication Patterns and Cognitive Differentiation." Mimeographed. Madison, Wisconsin: Mass Communication Research Center, University of Wisconsin-Madison, 1970.

Ward, Scott L. "Children and Promotion: New Consumer Battleground?" In *Social Marketing*, edited by W. Lazer and E. Kelly. Homewood, Illinois: Richard D. Irwin, Inc., 1973, pp. 423-436.

Ward, Scott L. "Consumer Socialization." Paper presented to the American Psychological Association Convention, Honolulu, Hawaii, 1972.

Ward, Scott L. "Consumer Socialization." *Journal of Consumer Research*, September 1974, pp. 1-14.

Ward, Scott L. and Gibson, David G. "Social Influence and Consumer Uses of Information." Paper submitted to Advertising Division, Association for Education in Journalism, Berkeley, California, August 1969.

Ward, Scott and Robertson, Thomas S. "Adolescent Attitudes toward Television Advertising: Preliminary Findings." Paper presented to the American Marketing Association Convention, September 1970.

Ward, Scott L. and Wackman, Daniel B. "Effects of Television Advertising on Consumer Socialization." Working Paper. Cambridge, Massachusetts: Marketing Science Institute, 1973.

Ward, Scott and Wackman, Daniel B. "Family and Media Influences on Adolescent Consumer Learning." *American Behavioral Scientist*, January-February 1971, pp. 415-427.

Ward, Scott; Wackman, Daniel; and Wartella, Ellen. *Children Learning to Buy: The Development of Consumer Information Processing Skills*. Report No. 75-120. Cambridge, Massachusetts: Marketing Science Institute, November 1975.

Ward, Scott; Wackman, Daniel; and Wartella, Ellen. *How Children Learn to Buy*. Beverly Hills, California: Sage Publications, 1977, pp. 134-135.

Williams, Joyce W. "A Gradient of the Economic Concepts of Elementary School Children and Factors Associated with Cognition." *Journal of Consumer Affairs*, Summer 1970, pp. 113-123.

Wolgast, Elizabeth H. "Do Husbands or Wives Make the Purchasing Decision?" *Journal of Marketing*, October 1978, pp. 151-158.

Zajonc, R.B. "Attitudinal Effects of Mere Exposure." *Journal of Personality and Social Psychology Monograph Supplement*, 1968, p. 1-27.

Zajonc, R.B. "The Process of Cognitive Tuning in Communication." *Journal of Abnormal and Social Psychology*, September 1960, pp. 159-167.